# EL CARACOL

## THE STORY OF ALFONSO

### Labor Camp Child

# EL CARACOL

## THE STORY OF ALFONSO

### Labor Camp Child

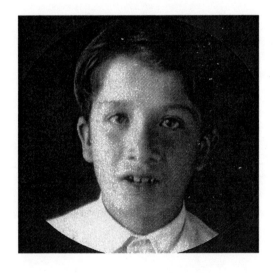

## YOLANDA ESPINOSA ESPINOZA

Mill City Press

Mill City Press, Inc.
212 3rd Avenue North, Suite 290
Minneapolis, MN 55401
612.455.2294
www.millcitypublishing.com

ISBN - 978-1-936400-58-4
LCCN - 2010938054

Cover Design by Wes Moore
Typeset by Madge Duffy

*Printed in the United States of America*

# ABOUT THE TITLE

I GAVE MUCH THOUGHT TO THE TITLE of this book about my father, Alfonso Cruz Espinosa. Toward the end of his life he wrote a poem entitled "El Caracol," which was an analogy of his life's journey. I was not immediately drawn to this phrase as a title for this book, however – in time – it became the only title that would do.

The Spanish word *caracol* has several definitions that parallel my father's story.

A *caracol* is a conch shell: a spiral shell that provides portable housing for a mollusk. The word "portable" stood out in describing the constant moving that was part of my father's life. Shells such as these have been used by people for ages as a rallying horn. The idea of a "rallying horn" captured my father's outspoken work for equality in his adult years.

A *caracol* can be a "winding staircase" or a "perilous journey." My father's life journey was certainly peppered with difficult and harrowing experiences. My grandfather referred to the Grapevine, the treacherous path from the Sierra Nevada Mountains into the San Joaquin Valley, as *"El Caracol"* that, in turn, inspired the title of my father's poem.

In the Hispanic world, a *caracol* is the winding mechanism that allows a watch or clock to keep precise time. This idea alludes to the indigenous concept of history being cyclical rather than chronological – an idea that my father found fascinating. His appreciation for the "story" of history prompted him to keep detailed notes and tapes documenting his life. I used these primary sources as I gathered information for this book.

And, most serendipitous, a *caracol* is a snail of the color periwinkle, a color whose name just happened to be the same as that of my grandmother Rita's favorite flower.

# ACKNOWLEDGEMENTS

THIS BOOK GREW FROM A MODEL LESSON that I created and presented for the California History–Social Science Project in 1994 at California State University, Bakersfield. After subsequent presentations, I received encouragement from fellow teachers to expand the lesson into a book. I thank them for that encouragement.

I must acknowledge the work of my aunt, Frances (Francisca) Espinosa, who wrote a detailed and poignant account of the lives of my paternal grandparents. Her book, *These Precious People,* provided me with much of the early history of my grandparents. Her exhaustive research of dates and places helped to fill in valuable missing pieces of my father's story.

I thank my sister Rosemary Edmiaston, my brother-in-law Jeff Edmiaston, and my daughter Aimee Espinoza for their honest and intimate feedback. Others who shared their invaluable time and suggestions include: Dr. Margaret Rose, Dr. Ronald Dolkart, Ms. Susan Chavez, Ms. Katherine Harper, Mrs. Christine Gonzalez, Ms. Rita Sluga, Mrs. Elsa Martinez, and Robert and Josephine Espinosa.

I thank my husband, Reynold Klent Espinoza, for his patience, encouragement, and assistance with computer technology.

I thank my children, daughters Deana and Aimee, and my sons, Mario and Matthew Espinoza, for their faith in me and their unconditional support. I am beholden to my grandchildren in whose eyes I see my parents smiling back at me.

I thank my students:  all those who spent part of their lives in my classroom inspiring me to be the best "story teller" I could be.

# TABLE OF CONTENTS

# PROLOGUE

## *No Spanish Allowed*

THE BLACK AND WHITE SIGN on the wall of the hospital ward called "Wayside" was well understood by the men, though they neither read nor spoke English: NO SPANISH ALLOWED. This ward was for the *Mexicanos* who had come to live their last days while the *tisico,* tuberculosis, ate away at their lungs. Alfonso eyed the sign warily. He was one of the few who could read the caustic words. The nurses who tended the men were uncomfortable with the foreign banter spoken among the men, and so they complained and got their wish – No Spanish Allowed.

Now the ward called Wayside at Springville Sanitarium was silent. In the late night hours, between the uncontrollable coughing fits that seemed to consume the skeletal bodies, there was silence. In the night,

1

orderlies would quietly remove a corpse from a bed and the ward would be steeped in a deeper silence. Too often, now, Alfonso would awake from a restless sleep to find the bed beside him empty. To him it seemed this ward had become like a tomb; the once jovial exchanges and reminiscences hushed.

One night, unable to sleep, Alfonso contemplated the effect that this decree had had on the *Mexicanos*. It seemed that the silence hurried them along to their death. Alfonso wanted to be able to talk to Miguel who was also nineteen and who had recently come from Mexico. He longed to reminisce with Señor Aguilar who had worked with Alfonso's father in the *algodón,* the cotton. These men knew almost no English but they needed to express themselves. To Alfonso it seemed that hearing and speaking the words about family and sweethearts and run-ins with *los jefes* was like healing ointment. Perhaps this verbal sharing could not heal his friends, but it could at least soften the nightmare of impending death.

What could he do? Who could he talk to about this injustice? He had heard that Dr. Winn was the chief physician and oversaw all the workings of the sanitarium, but would Dr. Winn listen to a nineteen year old boy who couldn't even walk a few steps from his bed without the help of a nurse? Would Dr. Winn listen to a boy who had dropped out of high school and whose only skill was chopping cotton and picking grapes?

Would Dr. Winn listen to a Mexican?

As soon as the early light seeped through the curtains, Alfonso summoned a nurse. The nurse looked perplexed when he told her he needed to see the chief physician. She shook her head incredulously as she helped him into a wheelchair and escorted him through the ward towards Dr. Winn's office.

As the wheelchair made its echoing approach down the cavernous corridor, Alfonso tried to calm the nerves that had oftentimes triggered a hemorrhage. The nurse tapped lightly on Dr. Winn's office door.

"Come in," came the stern, no-nonsense voice of the doctor.

Alfonso was wheeled into the office and Dr. Winn stared, surprised, at the young man.

The doctor's eyebrows came together at a furrow on his forehead and his lips were pursed. *Had he ever been visited by one of his patients? Not that he could recall.* Dr. Winn peered at the pale, emaciated young man and nodded for him to speak.

"Doctor Winn . . . doctor . . ." Alfonso stammered, suddenly feeling very tired. "Doctor,  I am Alfonso . . . I'm from Wayside . . . I am a *Mexicano* . . . but as you can see . . . I speak English." His sentences were short and choppy, his breathing shallow and winded.

Dr. Winn nodded acknowledgement and motioned for Alfonso to continue.

"The other men . . . they don't speak English . . .

Doctor, if you could please . . . try to understand . . . they are not allowed to speak . . . their language . . . and so . . . they don't speak at all . . . Doctor . . . . can you imagine not being allowed to speak?"

Before Dr. Winn could respond, Alfonso continued, afraid to breathe too deeply.

"Doctor, you know we are all dying. This disease . . . will take us all away soon.

My friends are dying but they can't . . . they can't share their fears . . . their stories . . . they are afraid to weep . . . or to laugh . . . because . . . it will surely be . . . in Spanish."

The furrow between Dr. Winn's eyebrows grew deeper. Alfonso sensed anger. What made him think he could sway this important man? Alfonso lowered his eyes.

"Please, Doctor Winn . . . our language . . . is all . . . we have left."

Alfonso dared not look up. Those few words had taken all his energy. He could hear the nurse's foot tapping nervously behind him. Dr. Winn stood and pointed toward the door. The nurse turned the chair around and wheeled Alfonso out of the office of the chief physician.

*My name is Alfonso and I have a story to tell you.*

*Before I left this world, my daughter, Yolanda, would share with me how concerned she was with many of her students who seemed to have lost their will to succeed. Many of her students seemed to care little about their lives or about their education. Many of them felt ignorant or inadequate. Some felt that no one cared about them. Some felt that no matter how hard they tried they would not be able to escape a bleak future. Some came from impoverished backgrounds and had few people in their own families to point the way for them. Some were neglected by their parents or lived with the knowledge that their parents were drug users or in prison.*

*Many of her students were migrant children, meaning that their families moved from place to place, working in fields or factories. These students found it difficult to feel welcomed in their schools. Some of her students were immigrants, meaning that they had come from other countries and felt like strangers and were sometimes ridiculed by others. Some were embarrassed about who they were or where they came from.*

*Some, however, were just lazy or were too busy doing things that were a waste of their time. They seemed to be going on a journey that would lead them nowhere.*

*My daughter believed that, perhaps, if her students heard my story, they might believe that they, too, could succeed no matter what challenges life put in their path; maybe her students would believe that they had a future and a hope.*

*When I was young I learned that history was a series of events, one event following another. Sometimes we humans learned from those events and sometimes we didn't. As I grew older, I preferred to look at history in the way many ancient cultures perceived it. They saw history as a spiral – a* caracol. *They believed that people and events would meet through time, in the stories and wisdom of their respective cultures. Sometimes the* caracol *would spiral up and sometimes it would spiral down, but if the ancients listened intently, they would be guided by those who had gone before them and they, in turn, would speak to those who followed.*

*I want to begin my story with the story of my own parents. I would listen to my parents' stories and found it hard to believe that they had survived their own childhoods. I marveled at the obstacles they had to surmount in order to survive, not only in the country of their birth but in their adopted country as well. Whenever I wanted to give up, whenever I felt awkward or ashamed or weak, I would think about all that my parents had endured and I would hear them whisper in my ear* "un paso más" *– one more step.*

*I now whisper in my daughter's ear as she sits at her computer and listens for my story. It is my hope that we meet in the pages of my story and that it helps you believe that anything is possible.*

# PART ONE

*The name I was given on the day of my birth was Alfonso Cruz Espinosa. I was named after my father. I listened to my parents' stories and remembered all that they told me.*

# 1

## *Las Estrellas / The Stars*

*EL OJO*. THE EYE. This is the name of the village where my father, Alfonso *Carrillo* Espinosa, was born in 1896. According to my father, it was a hard place – but beautiful in its dry desolation – in the desert mountains of *Chihuahua,* a state in northern Mexico. The natural spring that brought fresh water to the small town bubbled and flowed into the *Valle de Allende* where my father was born. My father was a good father but a hard father. He had lived a hard life and had struggled in poverty. He had been born into a family which consisted of nine brothers, a sister, and two parents who picked at the rocky ground to make their plot of land fruitful.

On sticky summer nights, sitting on the cool grass, gazing at the stars, my father would tell us children *cuentos,* stories, about his youth. He told those stories with so much clarity and emotion. Tears would come easily and so would the laughter as he described his early life.

He never went to school because there were few schools in Mexico at the time, especially for rural children such as himself. As a small boy he helped chop down trees and move stones to clear the land for planting. As a youngster, he plowed those fields with a team of mules. He sowed the seed and helped to harvest the corn. He chopped firewood, tended to the hogs and chickens, and milked the goats.

At the age of ten he was sent away for four years to live with his paternal grandparents and they sent the little boy into the hills to tend the sheep. He would be away for days, alone in the hills, wandering the ravines by day, sleeping under bushes and among the rocks at night. In the black stillness he would gaze into the coal-dark sky and stare, awestruck, at the cascade of stars twinkling in the black canopy above him. He would hug his tattered cloak close to his body in the stinging night air as huge tarantulas made their lazy treks across the darkened landscape. My father would grin, then chuckle, seeing our eyes open wide at the thought of those tarantulas as he described their furry silhouettes, making their nocturnal forays in the light of the moon.

He had been sent away because his parents had lost their land and could not feed their children. Sitting alone in the dark hills, singing songs to the stars, he would weep for his mama, Catalina, whom he loved and missed. She was a kind woman. He would see her face among the milky splash of stars, her green eyes and freckled face, her gold-brown hair and her sad soft smile. In the falling stars he would see her tears, her eyes glistening as he left his home, holding tight to the hand of his *abuelo*, his grandfather, Juan. As my father told these stories, I would peer up into his face as he stared into the stars and I would see that his eyes also glistened at the telling.

There were happy times for him, too, with his brothers riding their donkeys down to the *Rio Conchos*, splashing in the cool water on hot, thirsty days.

My father was born at a time when Mexico was on the brink of a great political and social upheaval. The president of Mexico, Porfirio Diaz, was a ruthless dictator who had an iron grasp on the land, taking land from the *peones*, the peasants, and handing it to foreign businessmen who sought only to leach what they could.

In 1910, these peasant landowners revolted and the Mexican Revolution began. After more than thirty years of omnipotent authority, the scoundrel fled, and Mexico was rid of Porfirio Diaz forever. However, most Mexicans continued to live in great poverty and were at the mercy of those who raced across the land, trying to establish their power, and taking advantage of the chaos and suffering. It was a nightmare time of whooping battle cries, firing squads, hunger and desperation. But as my father told these stories, I sensed that he saw the Revolution as a grand adventure and his eyes would twinkle like *las estrellas* above his head as he recalled those young riotous days in Mexico.

In 1913, when my father was seventeen, he became one of the *Dorados del Norte,* the "Golden Soldiers of the North," joining Pancho Villa's rag-tag but efficient revolutionary army. Pancho Villa led the insurgents in the northern states of Mexico and he was my father's hero – a man he admired from afar. My father would slap his leg and guffaw when he recalled some of Villa's infamous tactics. Villa didn't play war games by the rules. He thought nothing of mass execution of federal troops, but would bring trainloads of food to the starving inhabitants of northern cities. Villa was the Robin Hood of the downtrodden and when he was assassinated in 1923, my father composed an oral poem about the event:

*Pobre Pancho Villa,*
*fue muy triste su destino;*
*murió en una emboscada*
*a la mitad del camino.*

*(Poor Pancho Villa,*
*so sad his destiny;*
*he died in an ambush*
*in the middle of the street.)*

In 1918, a great catastrophe brought the whole world to its knees – the Great Influenza Pandemic. My father would quiet his usually gruff voice as he recalled the death of his youngest brother Francisco who had succumbed to *La Gripa*. Francisco, always happy and rambunctious, was only six when he took his last raspy breath and Mama Catalina wailed as she had with the deaths of her sons Salvador, Jesus, and Isidro that very same year. We children would get very quiet at the telling of this story. My father would take in the night air in a long breath and let out a sigh of memory as the crickets sang their songs to the moon and the owl chanted in the distance. We knew our father was very far away at that moment and no one dared interrupt his journey. And then he would chuckle and begin to tell us a story from the tales of the *Arabian Nights.*

These times under the stars were precious and few because my father worked hard in the fields to feed his growing family and these were the years of the Great Depression – a time when the economy of the whole world came crashing down. His weary head would sag, held by a hand pressed upon his forehead, and fatigue would press upon his shoulders. Then he would sit up straight and an animated expression would come to his countenance as he told of his adventures in the silver and gold mines of northern Mexico – *San Francisco del Oro* and *La Bufa* – located in the *Barranca del Cobre,* the mines of Copper Canyon. Those days in the mines were ruthlessly difficult and the labor beyond description.

Though the pay was piteously little, my father was thankful for that time because it was there where an exciting possibility began to unfold. It was there, in the darkness of the earth, that he began to look with the eye of the imagination, to the North – to that place across the desert from where stories of great opportunity were trickling into the imaginations of the young men of Mexico. These were restless young men eager to use their physical strength and tenacity to seek their fortunes in *El Gigante Del Norte – The Giant of the North* – The United States of America.

After a while, with the moon and stars still keeping watch over us, Mama would call us into the house. My father would tilt his head toward the house, nod, and with a *"vayanse,"* "Go!" we would quickly obey. We children would pile into one bed, wiggling and claiming our territory, but, almost immediately, sonorous breathing would fill the room. It was time to sleep and to dream and to wonder.

# 2

## *Los Ojos / The Eyes*

MY MOTHER'S NAME WAS RITA. She was the eighth child of Alejandra and Domingo Cruz. She was born in 1903 at the *hacienda* named *Villa de Santa Barbara.* This large ranch was also located in the state of Chihuahua.

The physical feature I remember most about my mother was her eyes. They were large and soulful and seemed perpetually sad. The sad-looking eyes were a physical trait inherent in the Cruz family, so that even when she was content my mother seemed sad. Later in my life I learned about a great sadness that my mother carried hidden in her heart. This sadness radiated through her eyes as she shared stories of her childhood with us. I would look intently at her face when she shared these stories and it seemed that she would narrow her eyes as

...d follow the Lord

to die to selfishness, our hearts will not be able to fully receive the glory our Lord wants us to experience.

## Lenten Action:

Resolve to examine myself for anything that blocks me from giving myself more fully to God in sanctity, and to pray for the grace to grow in simplicity, humility, and charity.

## Prayer Starter:

"O Lord, help me to live more simply and to desire greater sanctity, to be more and more clay in your hands"…

**Worship Schedule for Lent**

Mass Schedule

7:00 a.m.
8:30 a.m.   RCIA 3rd Scrutiny
10:00 a.m.
11:30 a.m.
5:00 p.m.
7:00 p.m.

Collecting for the Homeless:

**JUICE DRINKS & BOTTLES OF WATER**

if to look at something that was far away and obscured by shadows. I learned that, at the age of three, she had lost her own mother. Try as she might, she could catch only blurred memories of her mother, Alejandra Lazos. As a child, she always listened attentively when her older sisters would share snippets of their memories of the woman to try to learn more of her mother.

According to her sisters, their mother had been beautiful, with large green eyes, dark hair and an olive complexion. She had been born in Spain and was married to my mother's father at the age of fifteen. While braiding my mother's hair into *trensas*, her sisters shared stories of their mother's love of singing and embroidery. My mother would share how she could imagine her mother singing as she tended to the fragrant flowers in the garden of the *hacienda,* humming as she embroidered butterflies and birds on to the tablecloths and dish towels. My mother would imagine being held close to her mama, being rocked and hummed to sleep as loving fingers curled and caressed her baby tresses.

These were all imaginings, because my mother could not remember her mother. At the age of forty-one, my grandmother, Alejandra, had died giving birth to her last child. The tiny infant had been wrapped and buried beside its mother because it, too, had not survived. The following year, my mother's father, Domingo, married again, needing someone to help care for his children and the large estate that he oversaw.

My mother could remember being bad. At such a young age, not understanding the maternal absence, she could remember seeking the tender ghost in the many rooms and nooks of the sprawling house. She remembered pouting, kicking, and folding stubborn arms across her chest. Tomasita, her "new mother" would march her to the top of a nearby hill and tether her there under the harsh rays of the sun. My mother would sit and cry and pull at the scratchy twine that held her. She would slap at the ants that eyed her for a tasty meal. She threw pebbles at the scorpions as they sauntered her way. This was one of my mother's earliest memories.

My mother was born at a time when the Revolution had not yet set fire to Mexico and the Mexican people could not yet taste the sweet water of reform that would come many, many years after those tumultuous times. And so, my mother, like so many others of her time and place, never attended school. She never learned to read nor write and many years later she would sit at the table with my sister, Francisca, her fingers awkwardly wrapped around a pencil, cautiously forming the letters of her name.

My mother always put the cause of her darker complexion on the punishments she received, sitting atop the hill after her rebellious bouts. In fact, her father was of Aztec descent, with skin of cinnamon and jet-black hair, and so, in coloring, she was her father's child. She always spoke of her father affectionately and, although he was a very busy man – attending to the *hacienda* and providing for his children – he always found a moment to speak kindly to her, to caress her cheek, to smooth away a tear.

At the tiny age of five, my mother was put to work and she worked for the rest of her life. My grandfather was the overseer of the estate that was a typical *hacienda* of the time. My mother remembered the sweeping, scrubbing, polishing, folding, washing, and mopping in a continuous round of chores. The house consisted of an enormous kitchen and dining room, numerous bedrooms, a garden of herbs and fruit, a courtyard of flowering plants, and the perpetual altar to *La Virgen,* garlanded with flowers and flickering candles.

She and her sisters were always busy sweeping and mopping the tiled floors and attending to the piles of laundry after fetching heavy pails of water from the spring. After washing, they starched and ironed all the clothes, using *planchas* – heavy flatirons which had been heated on the wood-burning stove. At the age of nine, after her older sisters had married and left the house, my mother became the *mamacita* – the "little mother" of her younger siblings. Her proficiency at homemaking skills was to become her salvation and her curse. It would be her salvation because she would always be needed, put to work by her elder sisters and brothers as their own families began to grow. It would be her curse because she would be summoned, here and there, at the whim of those who assumed she was available to care for their needs.

My mother's oldest sister, Maria, had married and moved to El Paso, Texas. The wedding had been so joyful and the *hacienda* had come alive with music, flowers, dancing and reveling that had lasted for days. When it was time for Maria and her husband, Jesus Jose Santana, to leave, my mother held her sister close, fearing that she may never see her again, for in those days travel was very difficult and perilous. Few people could afford long journeys and most that left for far-away places never saw their families again. And so, my mother, Rita, held her sister for a long time before waving goodbye as the carriage disappeared along the dusty road.

Letters came to the *hacienda* with news of her sister's life in El Paso. My grandfather, Domingo, would gather his family around the kitchen table and in the flickering light of the lantern would read, with stops and starts, about the sad loss of several of Maria's babies. The family would listen with cautious hope when news of other babies came and pray that the delicate Maria was doing well and gaining strength.

One day a letter came that brought news that Maria was expecting another child and, a few days later, Jesus Jose arrived at the *hacienda* with an urgent request: Could Rita please return with him to El Paso to help Maria with the children and the new baby? "Absolutely not!" was my grandfather's reply. How could he let his little girl go so far away to tend to small children when she, herself, was yet a child? After much pleading from Jesus Jose, he reluctantly consented, but only under the condition that the stay be short.

In 1914, when my mother was eleven years old, she boarded a train and crossed the treacherous desert of northern Chihuahua to her destination in the United States. She could not have known that she would never return to the home of her childhood, nor see her father, again.

My mother stayed with her sister's family in Texas for eight years. During that time, when she was fourteen, she boarded another train and traveled to the mountains of Pueblo, Colorado, to her brother's home to help his ailing wife and children.

My mother would later describe the icy cold winter in Colorado, fetching firewood in the deep snow, and tending to her brother's five mischievous children. In the frigid night air, she would imagine the warm, sunny garden strewn with periwinkles in the *Villa de Santa Barbara*, and the festive gatherings around her father's table. She could imagine the dry beauty of the desert surrounding her home and the wildflowers that spread into the distance and blended into the distant mountains. Sometimes she would wonder, with a shiver of uncertainty, what her future held: Would she forever be the little handmaid, chasing someone else's children, cleaning someone else's home?

# 3

## *Hasta La Muerte / Until Death*

IT WAS RARE THAT BOTH MY PARENTS would sit with us children under the starry canopy of night. My mother usually stayed in the house tending to some chore and caring for the new baby, for there always seemed to be a new baby. Occasionally, she would join us under the stars as my father told his lyrical accounts of *Aladdin* and *Ali Baba* and she, too, would be mesmerized by the adventures. Sometimes, when my mother was present, my father would tell us the story of how they met. My mother would always protest, and we children would giggle and encourage our father to tell the story again for he told it with such drama and detail.

My father would always begin by retelling about his work in the mines of Copper Canyon and the eagerness with which he planned to migrate to the United States.

In 1918, after the death of his four brothers to influenza, his feelings of restlessness were more than he could contain. And, so, he and two of his brothers moved to Silver City, New Mexico, to seek their fortunes. At that time in history the border between Mexico and the United States was open and American industries aggressively recruited the *Mexicanos* who were a dependable work force.

My father would make short weekend trips to El Paso, a larger city on the border between New Mexico and Texas. On one such excursion he met and became enamored with a pretty young girl whose name was Maria de Refugio Santana. She was the eldest child of Maria and Jesus Jose Santana. He learned that her nickname was *Cuca* and that her grandfather was Domingo Cruz from the *Villa de Santa Barbara* which was in the vicinity of the *Valle de Allende*. My father would always share with us children how the *Mexicanos* found comfort in finding others in the United States who had emigrated from villages and towns that were in the same vicinity in Mexico. Knowing others from the same region helped to ease the loneliness and allowed for a sense of familiarity when reminiscing.

After a few attempts at courtship, my father asked for Cuca's hand in marriage, but an answer was delayed because she coyly procrastinated. Three times he proposed and three times she diverted his question. My father's face would harden at the telling of this part of the story and I could tell that his manly pride was ruffled by the memory. He would cross his arms across his chest, furrow his brow and explain that he had decided to give Cuca *one last chance* to accept his offer. He traveled to El Paso and delivered himself, all clean and shiny, to her parents' doorstep. He knocked on the door and Cuca immediately flew out and began to walk briskly down the street. But, before he could blurt out a word, she rudely commanded him to go inside *if* he was hungry, and then, without another word, she disappeared around the corner!

Humph! Not even a "hello" or a "goodbye!"

Rebuffed, my father decided to take up her offer of a meal and entered the house. He walked down the short corridor and into the kitchen. If he wasn't going to get an answer to his proposal today, he would, at least, fill his belly!

According to my father: *"When I entered the kitchen, the early morning sun filled the room with a brilliant ray of light."* He would dramatically squint and raise his hands to shield his face as he explained the scene. *"When my eyes adjusted, I saw a young lady dashing from the stove to the counter to the sink, then back to the stove. She seemed to have command of the kitchen and, wrapped in a colorfully-embroidered apron, crashed pans upon the stove, stirred whatever was in the pot and slapped* tortillas *on the* comal. *She nodded to me when I entered the kitchen but she was too preoccupied with her task to make a formal greeting.*

*"'Hello, good morning,' I said. 'Are you related to the family?'*

*"Without turning to face me, the young girl shyly responded in the affirmative, 'Yes, Maria is my sister.'*

*"'What is your name?' I confidently continued.*

*'My name is Rita,' she replied."*

My mother would always interject at this point in the story, describing how nosey my father seemed – wanting to know where she was from; what she was doing living there with the Santana's; and then asking the most presumptuous question of all: *"Are you married?"*

My mother would put on such a serious face at the retelling and say, "I don't know why he was asking me so many questions because I *knew* he was after my niece, Cuca!"

My father would always give my mother a wink at this point in the story and continue: *"'So . . . why is such a pretty young lady not married?'*

*'I suppose it is God's wish,' she replied as she slapped another* tortilla *upon the* comal.

*'Do you have a boyfriend?' I asked."*

My mother remembered that a hot flush had come upon her face when my father asked her that question and that she was glad that she was facing the stove and not this bold stranger. My mother was never too prideful to share these personal and intimate thoughts with us. She went on to describe the next part of the

23

story: *"I immediately regained my composure and answered him with an emphatic,* 'No!' *I turned and threw the* tortilla *into a basket on the table. What business was it of his to ask me such a personal question – and one I had often asked myself: Would I ever have a "novio?" I had felt so secluded from the rest of the world, always hidden away, so busy with the bidding of others. Would any young man ever come to court me in the hidden back rooms – to ask for* my *hand in marriage?*

*" 'No,' I said again only this time more gently. 'I do not have a boyfriend.'*

*" 'Oh, but you are mistaken,' was your father's immediate reply.*

*"Perplexed and somewhat irritated, I exclaimed that, no, I certainly did not have a boyfriend and that, after all, I should know whether I had a boyfriend or not! I remember kneading a small ball of* masa. *I thought about throwing the sticky dough at this rude young man but proceeded to pound it with the* palote. *I slapped it on the steaming* comal.

*" 'Well, you* do *have a boyfriend,' he countered, 'and he is in this very room!'*

*" 'Oh, really?' I exclaimed."* With much exaggeration, my mother would then put her hands to her waist and pretend that she was scoping the four corners of a tiny room. *"Then who* is *he?"*

My father would then stand up and straighten to the full six feet, three inches of his frame, bow deeply toward my mother and exclaim in his most proper Spanish: *"It is* I, *and* I, *Alfonso, am at your service. Will* you *marry* me*?"*

We children never got tired of hearing this story because it was so unbelievable. We would look at our father's face and then back to our mother's because we knew the rest of the story and wondered if it would somehow change over the years.

But it never did.

My mother once added to the story describing how she had turned to face my father at that moment, this man whom she had seen a few times from a distance when he had come courting Cuca. She remembered that morning in the kitchen as if it were beaming back from the cinema screen. She would describe the room being bright and warm. The aroma of *café de canela* and *frijoles al' olla* was wafting through the air. She remembered a sunray flitting upon my father's face and dust particles dancing in the room. She remembered blinking timidly into the hazel eyes of this tall young man who stared back at her with such sincerity and expectancy at the asking of this preposterous question. The room had become hushed as she peered shyly into my father's eyes and he into hers.

Just five minutes earlier she had been busily preparing breakfast for her sister's family. Just five minutes earlier she had been a servant girl, making a mental checklist of all the monotonous housework that made up her daily regimen. Just five minutes earlier she didn't even know this audacious young man.

*"Will you marry me?" he asked again.*

*"Yes," she quietly answered without hesitation, not believing that the word had just come out of her mouth but somehow knowing that it was said in truth.*

*My father extended his hand. She slowly raised her hand to grasp his. He shook it heartily and said,* "Hasta la muerte."

*And she responded,* "Hasta la muerte."

Now, as a grown man, I think about the story of my parents; where they came from and how they met, and I shake my head in astonishment. And, yet, I know that these stories are true because I know that my parents were honest people. I know also that they were married on September 20, 1922, at the Church of The Guardian Angel in El Paso, Texas. My father was twenty-five and my mother was nineteen when they married. And this I know for sure – they were together until death separated them.

# 4

## *Los Angeles / The Angels*

I DON'T REMEMBER BEING BORN, but I know that when I came into the world I was already wise and knowledgeable about a lot of things. This is something I would think about often: how we're born ready to understand everything and not knowing that we already know who we are and who we're supposed to be. It seems that life just fits around the crannies and folds we're born with; that life just molds itself around our destiny.

Before coming into this world, I floated quietly in the darkness. Seeping into my little mind were thoughts and feelings. Some were soothing and soft; some jolting and perplexing. I heard sounds and rustling, shouts and humming. At times I would hear the rhythmic pacing of a song: lyrics lilting, sometimes joyful, sometimes melancholy.

I remember, tucked in my little universe, the pat, pat, pat of my mother's heart. And, always, the rhythm would quicken in the silence and I would hear the voice calling to tiny voices and sometimes to a deep, gruff voice – a voice that would disappear into the day and return after the clanging of pots and pans, the rolling of the *palote* and the grating of the washboard. And then, again, the silence and the pat, pat, pat, and the soft, clear swooshing – and it was in this stillness that I would think about the meaning of all that had come into my mind. I listened and waited.

On January tenth, 1927, I was born. I was named after my father but was nicknamed 'Fonso. As a little boy, I would sit at the kitchen table, swinging my legs as my mother made *tortillas.* As she rolled the *palote*, she would tell me about the day I was born. She would remind me always that facts are not life. It wasn't until I was much older that I understood what she meant.

I was born on Lanfranco Street in the *colonia,* the neighborhood, of Boyle Heights in the city of Los Angeles, California. According to my mother, I was born refusing to cry. My little mouth was clamped shut but my nostrils flared with rhythmic breathing. My tiny fists were clenched and it seemed to her that I was thinking about something. It seemed to her that I was already saying to the world, "I am Alfonso!" Always, when she told me this story, she would glance over to me as I sat at the table and she would smile her sad smile.

In the years prior to my birth, many *Mexicanos* were migrating north from their *pueblitos,* villages, escaping the ravages of the Revolution. The U.S. border cities were becoming swollen with those seeking work. Because work was getting harder to find, my parents left El Paso after their modest wedding and made their way, by train, to California. California had become the new golden place of opportunity and many immigrants, including *Mexicanos,* were going there to look for work. My parents eventually settled in the bustling city of Los Angeles, in a tiny bungalow that held the bare necessities.

My mother would share stories about her trepidation about moving to the gargantuan city. Her anxiety was soothed, somewhat, after contemplating the name of their new home – *El Pueblo de Nuestra Señora, La Reina de Los Cielos y Los Angeles* – Los Angeles for short. If the city was built and named in honor of the mother of Jesus, "Our Lady, the Queen of Heaven and the Angels," then, in my mother's opinion, it would be a good place to settle. When I came into the world in 1927, my brothers Manuél and Roberto had already arrived. A year and a half after my birth, we were joined by my sister Francisca. We four children began our lives amid the clanging and whistles and honks and hammering of a thriving and growing city.

I was to learn later that my parents had a difficult time trying to feed and shelter our growing family. My father worked very hard to support us and the sometimes desperate days were relieved only by the proximity of *padrinos* and *paisanos* looking after each other in the crowded *barrios* of East Los Angeles.

My father again found work in underground caverns – no longer the mineral mines of northern Mexico, but now the water and sewer lines of Los Angeles. The work was unyielding and dangerous and, one day, my father did not return home at the usual time. My mother was frantic with worry when he did not return the next day, either. What had happened to him? she wondered in panic. Where could he be? How would she feed her children if her husband did not return? She had no skills, nor did she speak English! A candle was lit and set before *La Reina.*

My father finally did return several days later. He was bloodied, dazed, and hungry. He described to my mother the terrible accident that had occurred, at least what he could remember. As he worked in a trench, digging a line for new pipe, a huge metal tool slipped from somewhere above him and hit him on the head. He showed her the black, oozing wound above his forehead. He had been temporarily stunned and had fought unconsciousness. He had no recollection of where he had been for the last several days. He had simply walked away from the crew and had wandered, disoriented, until he had made his way back home. My father was weak and very sick for many days and I was to learn later that he had been fighting death. In those days, there was no help for people who were sick or injured or out of work. People had only their faith and the strength of their will to get them through such hardship.

My mother crossed herself as she always did when her *oraciones* to *La Virgen* had been answered, but her prayers were not strong enough to protect the baby that she was holding in her body. My brother, Salvador, was born on a rigidly cold day in late November only a few days after my father had found his way home. Because my father was so sick, my mother got herself to the hospital with the help of a neighbor. Babies were usually born at home in those days, but my mother sensed that something was not right. My brother was born too soon, and his tiny body could not fight the shivering sickness that overtook him. He died a week later and was buried in the cemetery near our home. He was buried in an unmarked grave in an area of the cemetery that was reserved for families who had no money to afford a proper funeral. Mama, however, saw to it that *el padrecito,* the priest from Santa Isabella Church, whispered the prayers for the dead over the tiny wrapped body and blessed the gravesite. I would wonder how Mama was able to leave that baby in the cold ground in that city that was so noisy and uncaring. Mama assured me that my baby brother was safe and warm and playing with *los angeles.*

# 5

## *El Caracol / The Grapevine*

I WAS FOUR YEARS OLD when my parents decided to join the migration to the great valley: *El Valle de San Joaquin*. The valley had been named in honor of Saint Joachim, the father of the mother of Jesus, and that was enough for my mother to reckon that the move could very well bring blessings to our family. So, after a heartfelt rosary and some more lit candles, we packed our sparse belongings and made ready to leave the City of the Angels.

I don't remember much about my life in Los Angeles, nor about the preparations to leave, but I do remember – as vividly as a four-year-old could – the wondrous horror of that journey to our new home. In the dark of the early morning hours, we were packed into my father's Dodge Brother, a vehicle that seemed impressive to me at the time, but must have been a tired piece of metal paid for with the few dollars my father had scraped together.

I remember sitting, cramped and scrunched, between my two brothers, with Papa and Mama in the front seat and Francisca on Mama's lap. We boys sat in the back seat on top of suitcases, boxes, and sacks filled with our worldly possessions. Mama was sad to leave some of the furniture they had acquired in Los Angeles, but she had refused to leave her treadle sewing machine behind. She called that machine *"La Segunda Madre"* and we children would have been hard-pressed to have clothing on our growing bodies if Mama had not insisted on strapping the "Second Mother" onto our already bulging vehicle.

As we turned north onto the highway, we were passed by other vehicles – including trucks – which caused my heart to pound as they chugged past our slowly-moving car. With the windows down, the air swiftly entered, circled, and exited, blowing our hair in a whirlwind and sounding like a continuous crashing wave. My father would begin to sing a song and the words would weave through the air and sometimes disappear into the billowing cacophony of wind, lumbering trucks, and blaring horns trying to bully us off the road.

We must have been a sight with our car piled with the precious belongings which my father had secured on the inside, outside, and topside. I know now that there were many more like us in the early years of the Depression – traveling like turtles with our homes strapped to our backs.

We crawled along the highway and I heard my father say goodbye to the city that he helped to build. I remember the wall of mountains which appeared in the far distance in the early sunlight, and my father pointing and telling my mother that the Great Valley lay beyond that wall. *"Ay! Dios mío,"* she whispered – more a prayer than an exclamation – and then her face took on a peaceful resolution that helped to settle my fear.

Our little car sauntered north along the narrow highway through the San Fernando Valley, chugging upward and into the mountains as the sun began to appear above the eastern horizon. The motor strained as we ascended those mountains and wobbled around the blind curves.

The highway narrowed into a two-lane path. I learned later that there were no guardrails at that time and that many cars had disappeared over the precipices before the new highways were built many years later.

Our car was dwarfed by the massive mountains, and the sun would appear and disappear – playing cat-and-mouse behind the towering sentinels. I would grab my mother's shoulder as the car made its struggling ascents, and I would press myself down and against the seat as the horizon disappeared. Then we would come to the top of an incline and Papa would press on the foot paddles and – at times – he seemed to stand on them because we were gaining speed on the descent and swift curves would appear out of nowhere.

The threadlike road seemed to wind and unravel as the treads of the tires screeched and skidded around the rounded summits of the San Gabriel and Tehachapi ranges. When the sun was full above us, I remember coming around a hilly curve to see soldiers staunchly marching over and down a hillside, descending in their armor with shields and spears and feathered helmets. Could they be a lost squadron of *conquistadores* that my father would describe in his exciting stories of *La Conquista,* the great Conquest of Mexico? I blinked and realized that they were not Spanish soldiers, after all, but some strange plant which my father called *yuca* that grew scattered across the mountainous landscape.

I saw cows and bulls grazing in the meadows and in the shade of *los robles* that I would later learn are called "oak" in English. And I remember the shimmering, green-gold willows that grew along the creeks and rivulets, their sequined leaves glittering in the pristine sunlight. Flowers of orange, purple, and yellow seemed to have been sifted, haphazardly, onto a rolling carpet of green.

I remember the jutting rocks, the canyons and ravines, and the evergreens at the higher elevations, and the air – fresh and cold – swooshing through our car and Mama shivering. And then, after many hours of traversing the ridges and valleys, I saw something that took my breath away and I heard a collective gasp from my mama and brothers. A glimpse – wedged between the steep sides of the mountains – of a great, wide, flat expanse appearing, extending and disappearing into the haze of the horizon. My father stopped the car. We tumbled out. I held tight to Mama's hand as she held tight to Francisca. She called to Manuél and Roberto to stay close and we peered in silence at the endless valley that spread before and below us.

*"El Valle,"* my father whispered. *"El Valle San Joaquin!"*

As we were perched there at the top of that high ridge, the vision of that valley became etched in my memory as a gaping mouth ready to devour us.

I would later imagine the thought that must have been whirling through my parents' minds: How would our little family make it down the treacherous descent? I saw my mother cross herself and whisper her prayer to the Holy Family, *"Jesus, Maria, y Jose,"* as we scurried back into the car. We would have to get down to the valley floor before sunset.

I would learn later that the horrendous downward portion of that highway was called *El Caracol,* the "Grapevine," named for the grape-like ivy that clung, stubbornly – desperately – to the rocks and boulders on the mountainsides along the highway. Named, too, I'm sure, for the spiral tendrils of those vines and the tendril-like ribbon of road that would deliver us to our destination.

Again there was the screeching of brakes, the grinding of the clutch, and the silence within the thunderous fear in our hearts. Again the twists and turns, the curves and cliffs, the winding ascents and careening descents and finally . . . miraculously . . . the velvety, bulbous arms of the hills gently laying our family down upon the valley floor.

Our little car continued along the highway, sputtering and heaving. But now the landscape was flat, and I remember the verdant green of the vast, dry wasteland, dusted with purple wild flowers.

The wind continued to whip its way through the car, but now it was warm and I remember the fragrance: sharp and green. Orchards and neatly-striped rows of grapevines began to appear sporadically along the highway.

I must have fallen asleep for a short while, and when I awoke the sun was slowly dipping behind the western mountains and tiny lights began to flicker in the far hills to the east and west and on the far horizon to the north. My eyes were heavy and I glanced up at my mother who was asleep with Francisca snuggled in her arms. I could hear my brothers snoring on either side of me. I turned toward my father and his eyes were resolute upon the road, a slow whistled tune sifting through his teeth. I sat up on my knees and faced behind me to the dark mountains from where we had come.

We had survived *El Caracol*, as my father called it, and later I thought about my father and what he must have been thinking: What harrowing challenges would he find at the end of this highway? Would he find work? Would he be able to feed his family? Would he find respite from the endless physical labor that he could not seem to escape? But those were not my worries and I snuggled back into the seat and drifted away again, lulled by the whirring of the motor, knowing I was safe and that all was well.

In my later years, I would think back to that journey to the Great Valley. I would remember the fear that had caused my heart to race and the dread that burrowed in the hollow of my throat. But always I would recall the faith of my parents: my father with his hands tightly wrapped on that steering wheel knowing that somehow the brakes would hold, and my mother with her whispered prayers and her eyes clenched shut with visions of angels hovering about her.

I knew that wherever my journey took me, I could take one step at a time, round one treacherous curve at a time, climb and tumble down, peer at certain death and then take *un paso más*. I knew that, somehow, I would arrive at the place that destiny had already chosen for me.

# 6

## *La Niebla / The Fog*

I AWOKE IN A STRANGE ROOM, but any fear I might have felt was soon relieved by the aroma of eggs frying and the soothing smell of *tortillas* and *café* and the deep, rich laughter that I recognized to be my father's. We had safely arrived at the home of my father's brother who had encouraged my father to leave Los Angeles and join him, assuring him that there was much work in the orchards and fields of the San Joaquin.

And so it was that in the spring of 1931, we made our first home at a labor camp in the outskirts of McFarland, California. How was I to know at that time in my life that this place would be the beginning of a seemingly endless trek from town to town, camp to camp, house to house? How was I to know that I would someday liken myself to Odysseus and that those rich adventures that my father so aptly relayed would become for me, not a glorious – but a tiresome – journey?

I remember one warm morning, as I swung my legs at my mother's table and sipped a warm *atole*; we were having one of our conversations about whatever I wished to talk about. She would pause her gentle humming to answer one of my endless questions. I don't remember our topic but I remember that she excitedly exclaimed, *"Gracias a Dios, 'Fonso! Gracias a Dios!"*

"Thanks be to God that we have friends and family. There are many here in the Valley who have nothing. There are some who have no one, and they have nowhere to go," she explained in her lilting Spanish.

I looked at her, wide-eyed, because I could not imagine people with nothing, no one, and nowhere to go.

*"Los Okis,"* she said, and shook her head. I didn't know at that time who *Los Okis* were, but my mother's sad eyes and the slow undulation of her head compelled me to have much concern for these people who had nothing, had no one, and had nowhere to go. There were many times that we would be traveling along a country road, Papa at the steering wheel, Mama with a baby in her arms, us children rabble-rousing in the back seat, and we would come upon small bands of people camped along the creeks and canals, or tents strung to tree limbs.

There would be rickety cars piled high with mattresses, pots and pans, and large buckets. I would see children with white-wild hair and red faces, running barefoot. Bony men with desperate faces would be standing around and women at the fires, staring, empty-eyed, into the iron frying pans. Mama would never stare at these people because it would be rude, but I gazed at them in awe and would whisper ever so quietly, *"Los Okis."*

My mother was right about the Okies. But she was also wrong. She was right when she said that they had nothing. I was to learn later in my life that the Okies had left their homes and land in a far-away part of this country because the wind had blown away the good soil and nothing would grow in the dusty soil left behind. The powdery dust buried their land, their homes and their dreams. So they packed their few belongings and came to the Great Valley.

Mama was right when she said that they had no place to go because the people of the Great Valley didn't want them there. *Los gabachos*, as my parents called the white folk, were embarrassed by the miserable poverty of the Okies. Because the Okies would work for practically no pay, wages went down, even lower than they already were. I guess any man would work for practically nothing if his children were starving. The Okies always had to keep moving because if they stayed in any one place too long they were scolded away like vagrant dogs.

But Mama was wrong about the Okies having no one. They had their families and they had each other and they had their faith. Then again, she was right because she always said that the good God was always looking out for His creation and she believed that the Okies were certainly part of His creation. I learned compassion at my mother's table. I would think about how some people suffer much and can become bitter and hateful and how others suffer just as much but can have so much understanding for others who have suffered in the same way.

Many years later as I traversed those same country roads, I could see the misty ghosts of those people. Some had disappeared as if into the thick Tule fog – that vapor that seeps up from the reeds and rushes of the valley floor. Family names have been forgotten – erased from memory. But some had survived and overcome the dismal days of the Great Depression. They had blended into the thriving life of the Great Valley despite the hatred they had suffered.

# 7

## *El Paraíso / The Paradise*

OUR FAMILY FOUND TEMPORARY HOUSING in a small shack by the railroad tracks on the east side of McFarland. This area was the *colonia* where all the *Mexicanos* lived. At this time in my life I didn't know that people of different nationalities or races separated themselves in neighborhoods with others like themselves.

Our "house" consisted of a one-room enclosure with a dirt floor and a wood-burning stove. Mama was not happy with this arrangement and, thankfully, we soon moved to the Weller Ranch. The Weller Ranch was owned by a man named Mr. Earle Weller who farmed grapes, peaches and almonds. He had built five structures to accommodate some of his workers. My uncle helped my father secure a job with Mr. Weller, so we packed our belongings and traveled a short two miles west of McFarland on Perkins Road to the Weller Ranch.

The shack we settled into was quite small, consisting of two rooms with no electricity or running water. One of the rooms had a wooden floor and it was in this room that we all slept. The kitchen had a dirt floor and a wood-burning stove for cooking and heating. Each house at the camp had an outdoor latrine located a distance away. The latrine consisted of a hole in the ground covered by a wooden box. This box was covered by a lean-to with open slats and knot holes and spider webs laced the corners.

I don't know how Mama felt about our home at the Weller Ranch, but for me it was located in some kind of paradise, isolated in the middle of grape vineyards and orchards, with a great pond called a "reservoir" near the road.

Soon after our arrival, my two brothers were enrolled in school and I became my mother's helper. Early in the morning, after my father had already left for work and as my brothers washed and dressed for school, I assisted her in the kitchen. I helped to pack the lunches, serve the *avena,* clear the table, and wipe the dishes. The yellow school bus would tumble down the country road and honk from a distance. Manuél and Roberto would race out the door and not return until late afternoon.

I treasured this quiet time alone with Mama as she made a stack of *tortillas* and I sat at the kitchen table with my bowl of warm cereal. I remember having so many questions for her. I was always wondering about how things worked and why things were. She always seemed to have an answer for me and sometimes, when something just seemed too illogical or unfair, she would nod her head and say, *"Así es porque así es."* As a boy, this explanation that "things are such because that's the way things are" seemed to make perfect sense, and I would nod my head in agreement.

New babies arrived. Arturo was delivered as a Christmas present on December twenty-third in 1931. Twins arrived in 1934, and Alícia and Alfredo kept Mama very busy. Mama shared later that Alfredo was a real surprise. Alícia had been born first, and no one realized that another baby was on the way. Hours later, when Alfredo decided he was ready to be born, his arrival shocked everyone, including Mama, though she said she had a feeling that something more was going to happen. Alfredo was born very tiny and weak and the doctor told Mama not to even bother to feed him because he would not survive. Of course, Mama knew that only God decided such matters, and she fed and cuddled the baby and soon his bony little face got pudgy and he would let us all know that he was hungry because his face would turn red with his insistence.

One of my fondest memories of that time on the Weller Ranch was the friendship I made with Guiri.

Guiri was a slight Japanese man who lived in one of the little houses in the labor camp and tended to Mr. Weller's strawberry plantings. Guiri would spend most of the day working on the rows of strawberries and, in the early summer, fat sweet berries would miraculously appear. These would then be sold in the nearby communities but only after we children had had our fill of the harvest. For several days, our lips would be bright red from the berry stain and Mama would have to brew tea from the *hierba buena* – a minty medicinal plant that grew wild around the irrigation standpipes. She would use this tea to soothe our digestion problems after our gluttonous sampling of strawberries.

Guiri was always smiling, though he hardly spoke. His hand gestures were clearly understood and he must have understood bits of our Spanish as we tried to decipher his Japanese. Occasionally, on Saturday mornings, he'd come knocking at our door and announce "pancake" and we children would run to his house and devour his delicious pancakes smothered in fresh butter cream and the homemade molasses that he kept in a barrel on his back porch. Of course, Mama always shared samplings of her delicious cooking, and many times I was sent to Guiri's house with a cotton towel neatly-rolled, containing *taquitos de carne* and *burritos de huevo* or, during Lent, Mama's *capirotada,* her delicious bread pudding.

One morning, as I sat at the kitchen table, I remember

Mama telling me that Guiri must be very lonely. She told me that he was far away from his family who lived in a very far-away land and she shook her head with those sad eyes and I remember feeling very sad for Guiri. Sometimes, after chores, I would walk behind Guiri as he walked the rows of strawberries just to keep him company. I would chase butterflies and collect June bugs as Guiri pulled weeds and caressed the tiny sprouts. When the berries were ripe, my family would help pick them on weekends. I remember Guiri showing me how to pick good berries and how to pull them properly and then gently place them in small canisters.

Once a month, on a Saturday, my father would pack us all, including Guiri, into the Brother and we would go into Delano – to Honda's Grocery Store – to do the shopping for staples like flour and sugar. My father would then go to the *cantina* to visit with his *paisanos* and we older children would go to *el cine* with Guiri. Mama would stay in the car, sometimes into the night, with the younger children. It didn't occur to me at the time, but later I wondered how my mother could stay in that car so long with those tired, rambunctious babies while Papa went to the tavern and we went to the cinema.

The movies were always in English and we didn't understand the dialogue but we could clearly understand the action. We children would whoop and holler, and Guiri would get all excited right along with us.

One day Guiri disappeared. His little house was

empty and the molasses barrel had been washed and stood empty on the back porch. His abrupt parting was a mystery.

Later, Papa came home with some bad news: Guiri had boarded a ship bound for Japan and somewhere along the way, in the middle of the Great Ocean, he jumped overboard and disappeared into the swells. When I asked Mama why Guiri, who was so kind and good, would do such a thing, she answered that sometimes things were such simply because they were.

I learned, later, that many Japanese were returning to their native land because of rumors of war between their country and the United States. Some time later, this rumor would become a fact. When World War II began years later, many Japanese were forced to leave this country. In fact, many United States citizens of Japanese ancestry would be forced to leave their homes and be relocated to isolated camps in the deserts right here in the United States. They had become "prisoners of war" even though they were good and hardworking people – like Guiri.

My uncle, too, decided to take his family back to Mexico because his sons were older and he was getting increasingly uncomfortable with the threats of a great war. My father, however, had no such concerns and our young family thrived during our days at the Weller Ranch.

A memory that has remained most vivid for me was the weekly wash day. Because I was the eldest at home after my brothers left for school, Mama would send me to the standpipe to fetch water for the *tina,* her wash tub. I would climb the ladder that leaned against the standpipe and dip my bucket into the dark cavernous cylinder. Later in my life, I could visualize myself teetering on that ladder on the rim of the standpipe and would have to thank Mama's prayers for the fact that I never fell in, for I would have surely drowned. Back and forth I would trudge with my bucket splashing and swaying, and by the time I arrived at the large *tina,* half the water would have escaped the bucket. My sister Francisca would try to help, but she was so tiny, she would usually drop her bucket and start crying in frustration. So back and forth I went until Mama had all the water she needed to wash and then rinse all the clothes for the family.

For what seemed like hours, on cold winter mornings or sweltering hot days, Mama would stand at the ribbed surface of the washboard, rhythmically grating those clothes up and down, suds splashing over the side of the *tina.* I would then help Mama hang the clothes on the *tendero* by handing her the clothespins. If it started to rain or if a dust storm was whipping up, she would call out to me to help her: *"Andale, 'Fonso, ayudame!" (Hurry, 'Fonso, help me!")* Off we'd go to fetch the laundry from the lines.

We were never hungry while we lived on the

Weller Ranch. Mr. Weller appreciated my father's skills and his willingness to work from sunup to sundown. Even after the harvest – when other families were forced to move on – my family had a roof over its head and food on the table. We were free to collect the bounty that surrounded us: peaches, apricots, quince, almonds, grapes, strawberries, watermelon, cantaloupe, boysenberries, potatoes, corn, oranges, squash, sweet potato, and the sweet *hierba buena* that would permeate the air when picked. Papa kept a small garden on the side of the house and planted tomatoes, chili peppers, turnips, onions, and carrots. I remember Mama in the steaming kitchen, with Francisca and Alícia at her side, cooking and storing Papa's harvest in the hot jars she had prepared for canning.

There were catfish and turtles in the nearby pond. There were pigs, chickens, goats, turkeys, and a thousand ducks. The chickens, ducks, and turkeys would raise all kinds of ruckus when Mama went into the yard at feeding time with her *"pio, pio, pio."* More birds would come flying from the farther side of the reservoir creating the most wonderful commotion. Then *los perros y los gatos* would come alive from their naps with their barking and mewing, for somehow they knew they were next to be fed. Sometimes we would catch the hungry eyes of a *coyote* watching from a distance, with envious eyes and a watering tongue, upset that he could not join in the feast.

On weekends and during the summer months, before we boys had to go to work in the fields, Manuél, Roberto, and I had what I would later describe as the perfect childhood. After chores, our days were filled with play – play to the limits that our imaginations would take us. We would reenact those vivid cinematic episodes starring The Lone Ranger, Zorro, Tom Mix, Rin Tin Tin, and Johnny Mack Brown. The willow tree that dropped its limbs over the reservoir would become the deepest jungles of Africa as we became Tarzan swinging from its "vines." We would be shipwrecked and "lost" like Robinson Crusoe, wandering throughout the tiny labor camp, trying to find our way back home in time for dinner. We would reenact the exploits of Sinbad with our homemade swords and magic powders. Francisca would try to keep up with us boys and would get toppled over, pushed, poked, pummeled and – one time – would nearly have drowned if Roberto had not come to her rescue.

We made rafts and explored the far reaches of the world in that reservoir. We would climb the highest mountain which just happened to be the side of an old barn, and then jump into a hill of hay to escape the pursuing hordes. We'd go hunting with our homemade slingshots. We hunted snakes, frogs, squirrels, rabbits, lizards, and birds. We were always in motion: running, jumping, swimming, swinging, crawling, climbing, chasing, or dodging. Then we would rest in the shade of *los alamos* – the cottonwood trees – or under the willow by the reservoir as a cool breeze whipped across the water and we'd tell stories or make up riddles. And, on summer evenings, when the house was still hot from the stove fire, we'd sit under the stars as Papa shared his wonderful *cuentos*.

Though this time in my life seemed idyllic, I would later wonder about the conditions we truly lived in. As a boy, I remember thinking that Mr. Weller was some kind of god. After all, he allowed us to stay in our home and kept Papa employed. Yet, in my mind's eye, I can still see Mama stuffing the slats and knotholes in the walls with paper and rags and swatting scorpions and large spiders that squeezed through the floorboards. I remember the constant swatting of *mosquitos* and the large itchy welts that scarred our bodies. I can still see our frightened faces as *coyotes* or bobcats came sniffing around the perimeter of our home at night. In the winter it seemed we were always shivering after the heat of the woodstove had blended into the frigid air. We children would cuddle close for warmth as we snuggled under the threadbare blankets.

During rainstorms water would steadily drip from the ceiling as Mama placed pans in strategic places. Wind would whip through the house during storms and dust would seep through the sideboards. Sometimes we'd huddle under sheets to keep the dust from filling our nostrils. In the sweltering summer months we had only nature's sporadic breezes to cool the house. Because Mama still had to get the stove burning for cooking, the house would become unbearably warm and we children would spend most of the day playing outside or under the shade of *la mora,* the mulberry tree. Mama, however, had to spend most of her day inside and I remember her fanning a sick baby with a wet towel while beads of sweat dripped from her own face. And I remember the absence of my father and his stooped shoulders as he trudged home with his lunch pail in the late evening.

Though we lived in the meekest of conditions, I was buoyed by the music that permeated the home life of my childhood. Mama always hummed and sang as she worked. Papa was always whistling and would break out in spontaneous song. The words of those songs taught me so much about the culture and language of my people, *los Mexicanos.* I realized later in my life that these songs about love and love lost, of longing for a far-away home, of great quests and sad failures, were the songs of all people and of all cultures – only the language was different.

One summer morning, I awoke in bed and the sheets were already wet with sweat and my hair was plastered onto one side of my face. The house was unusually quiet. I saw that my brothers and sisters were still asleep, sprawled helter-skelter on the floor and bed. I quietly got out of bed and saw Mama standing at the window, the gauzy curtains weakly moving in the breeze. I stood there watching her for what seemed the longest time. She stood immobile except for the slow soft sway of her head as a haunting tune swelled almost inaudibly from her throat: "*Una paloma blanca tiende su vuelo hacia al sol, y mi corazón no lá olvidará . . .*" ("*A white dove stretches her flight toward the sun, and my heart will not forget her . . .*")

My mother turned and saw me. Her eyes were filled with tears.

I never asked her why she was crying. I knew that this was a moment that she and I would forever keep between us. Later in my life, contemplating this moment, I realized that as Mama faced that window, she was facing south. She was facing toward the home of her father. She was facing toward the home of her innocence, her childhood, so very far away in time and distance.

Those precious days of my childhood were to come to an end. In my own innocence, and ignorance, I believed that life would always be safe and good. I would be leaving the security of my mother's side where I had already learned so much about life. I would be leaving that morning table where I had learned that I was unique. I was going to a place where I would learn that "*así es porque así es.*" I would learn, too, that I would no longer be satisfied with that reality.

# PART TWO

# 8

## *Escuela / School*

I DON'T KNOW HOW OLD I WAS when I started to notice the cold. In the dark mornings of late fall and winter Mama would awake and get the stove burning. I don't remember actually seeing her get out of bed but I knew that sometime before we children awoke, she had already collected firewood from a pile outside the door and gotten the fire roaring. When my eyes would sleepily open, I could hear the stumps and broken branches crackling in the stove and I could see little fingers of smoke curling into the frosty air. From my warm place in the bed, I could smell the aroma of coffee that she prepared for my father – who would disappear into the darkness and not return until the sun was setting.

After my father's departure Mama would rally us out of bed and our morning ritual would begin. We older children would wash from the *tina* in the warm water that Mama had prepared. Mama would then attend to the younger children as they awoke, crying and cold. We would still be shivering and rubbing our bare arms for warmth as Mama handed us clean clothes for the day. Soon enough, the kitchen would be warm and Manuél and Roberto would be dressed, fed, and out the door for school as the sun was peeping over the horizon.

One morning, I awoke to find my father sitting at the kitchen table sipping his coffee. Mama called me to the *tina* and commenced to give me a good scrubbing, then handed me a new pair of store-bought pants and a shirt. This was quite surprising, since new clothes – and especially store-bought ones – were something we rarely saw. Mama cleaned my ears and combed my hair. I kept very quiet and didn't ask any questions because I could sense that something was amiss. Mama did not look happy and it seemed that she was ready to burst into tears. After I was scrubbed, dressed and combed, she took me by the shoulders, looked into my eyes and told me that today I would be going to school. I remember shaking my head and wondering why. I didn't want to leave the warm kitchen where I had always helped her prepare the morning meal.

The school year had already been in progress for several months and why my parents did not enroll me at the beginning of the school year, I will never know. I do know that my father drove me to school in the town of McFarland that morning in 1933 and marched me into the kindergarten room. The teacher approached us and, after having a short conversation with my father, pointed down the hall. I was to learn later that – because I was almost seven years old – I was too old for kindergarten; and, so, my father escorted me to the first grade classroom.

As we walked down the open hall, I remember keeping my head down, counting the spaces between the wooden planks of the floor as my stomach churned with dread. I felt clumsy and embarrassed. I was afraid of being left at that school, but knew that my father would not tolerate any show of cowardice. I tried hard to keep up as he walked ahead of me with his long steps. I wanted to grab onto his leg and not let go.

But I also felt excited. For one thing, I knew that somewhere at this school my brothers could be found if needed. And in those few short minutes when my father spoke to the kindergarten teacher, two things occurred to me. First, as I peered into that room I noticed the bright colors, shapes, and smells, and something seemed to jump in my stomach with anticipation. I noticed jars of paints and brushes. I saw a large board, painted black, with letters and drawings scrawled upon it. But, also, as I heard the teacher talk to my father, I realized that the words she spoke were very different than the words my father and mother spoke. They sounded like the words I heard at the cinema, and it occurred to me that I actually understood some of the things she said to my father.

The door to the first grade classroom was closed. My father knocked on the door and a few seconds later the door opened. There stood the most beautiful woman I had ever seen. Miss Miller smiled at me, spoke briefly to my father, and then took me by the hand. She led me to a desk and then motioned to my father that he could leave. I remember being mesmerized by the room as I shyly looked about me. Some children turned toward me and kept staring. I tried to ignore them as I perused the walls covered with bright posters, charts, and maps. There seemed to be a thousand books neatly stored in the open cupboards. And, again, the large black board with white markings and drawings.

Miss Miller called me to the front of the room where I stood as she introduced me to the class and proceeded to ask me some questions. I remember just staring at her and I could sense that she understood that I did not understand a word she was saying. Little did she know that I actually *could* comprehend some of her words but I didn't have a clue how to respond. I knew that she wanted me to answer in her language, but I didn't know her language. My lips felt pasted together, and I sensed that if I responded in Spanish the children would probably burst out laughing. I know that my face must have turned as red as a beet and – if she had not motioned for me to return to my desk – I believe I would have peed in my brand new pants.

A few minutes later, I actually did pee in my pants. I didn't know how to ask to use the latrine and was too embarrassed to ask this beautiful lady such a personal question. I remember sitting there, wiggling, feeling like I was ready to burst, and then I just let it go and the urine went down my pant legs and started to create a puddle on the floor. Several children started to giggle, and soon it seemed that the whole class was pointing and giggling. I was so ashamed I wanted to cry.

I did cry.

Miss Miller walked over to me and patted my shoulder and mumbled some words to me while she raised her hand over her head. I understood that she was showing me how to get permission to leave the room. Thankfully, she didn't have me get up, then and there, to parade myself out.

Some minutes later, a loud buzzing noise made me jerk in my seat and I noticed the children get noisy and restless. I later learned that what I had heard was called the "recess bell." When the children had emptied out of the classroom, Miss Miller came to me, took my hand, and led me outside. She walked me to the end of the hall and pointed to a small building that had the silhouette of a running boy on the door. She was so kind and smiled at me with a smile that seemed to say that she understood how I must be feeling. It was then that I noticed her eyes. They were blue. I must have stared into those strange eyes a moment too long, because her smile got even wider and she pointed again to the building.

I walked to the small building and looked inside. The room was dark and smelled awful, but then I saw some white tubs that were attached to the floor. Each tub had a string that dangled from the ceiling with a handle attached to it. I stood at the entrance, confused about what I was seeing, when a door swung open and a boy bolted out with a whirling noise behind him. He ran out of the building and I walked to the tub and saw water swirling down. I remember feeling like I had discovered a grand treasure when I realized that this was a toilet! I stood over the tub and pulled the cord and, sure enough, the water swirled and then disappeared. I pulled the cord several more times. Home was not like this. Here you just pulled the cord and the whole mess would disappear! This was an incredible discovery. I could hardly wait to get home to tell Mama all about it.

I pulled that cord several more times before I heard the loud buzzer again and realized that I probably should get back to the classroom. I pushed open the wooden door and began to cross the dark damp room, when a boy entered. He was tall and wore tattered blue-striped over-alls. My immediate reaction was fear – for he turned toward me and stared me down with his pale, red-rimmed eyes. His face was long and freckled. A thick patch of red hair looked as if it had been pasted to the top of his head.

"Mexican!" he hissed.

The word splattered out of his mouth and spit dribbled from his teeth. His eyes were fixed on mine.

"Dirty Mexican," he hissed again.

I walked slowly toward the door and watched his fists clench and open, clench and open.

I didn't know the word "hate." That emotion had had no reason for being a part of my life up to that day. I learned the word that day through the clenching of the fists and the red-rimmed eyes brimming with something I did not know but somehow understood.

I walked into the cold, open hallway and could feel his hate follow me. I did not look back, but walked in a daze to the bench in front of the classroom and sat there, my feet rhythmically swinging. A frigid breeze caressed my face and I thought of my mama's warm, calloused, fingers soothing my face after a fall; gently smoothing away little-boy tears. I looked out into the schoolyard and across into the orchard beyond the access road. A thin blanket of late morning fog draped the lanes between the trees. I knew that, beyond the field and the trees, beyond the frozen land that would soon be alive, Mama would be washing clothes in the *tina* under the bare branches of *la mora*. And I was not there to help her.

A draft whistled through the rafters.

*Mexican.* What was that word? I did not know then what I someday would. I would forever associate that word, the hard harshness of its syllables, with hatred.

I would learn, also, that it was a version of a word I knew well – a word that meant family and laughter and music and tears: *Mexicano,* the melodic word that was my identity.

I felt a gentle tap on my shoulder. I turned and there stood Miss Miller. She smiled and stretched her hand toward me. I took her hand and stood. By then, the breeze had helped to dry the pee that had mapped itself on the front of my trousers. She led me back into the classroom and to my seat. I settled in, ignoring the snickers, and proceeded with my education.

I was a fast learner. The first lesson I learned was that the language I used in my parents' home was strictly forbidden at this school. The second lesson I learned was that I would not be easily accepted by many of the children. In fact, the playground became a battleground and I was the enemy. I quickly joined forces with another *Mexicano*, by the name of Pete Ramirez, who I nicknamed "Pito Pitoche," and a Negro boy named Leroy. Leroy came up to me one day on the playground and started to follow me around. I had never seen someone with his coloring before, and I felt somewhat perplexed by his attention, not sure what to make of him. He called me "Pooncha."

As Pito Pitoche, Leroy, and I ran and jumped and played our recess games, we were always on the lookout for those gangs of boys who would taunt us and call us names. Pito and I were called "greasers", "dirty Mexicans," and "pepper bellies." Leroy was called "nigger."

One day, while I was in second grade, Leroy ran up to me from out of nowhere all dusty and bloody; blood and tears dripping from his nose, mouth, and eyes. He called out, "Pooncha, Pooncha, he beat me up!"

"Who beat you up, Leroy?" I asked in my stuttering English, starting to feel all agitated and angry.

Immediately, Leroy recoiled and started to shake his head as if to say *never mind.*

"Tell me, Leroy. Show me who did this."

Leroy pointed to a group of boys who were looking our way, and the red-headed boy, whom I had encountered in the toilet room, glared back.

I'm not sure what came over me. I knew I was tired of feeling afraid of those boys. I knew that I felt stupid and weak when I purposely looked for ways to sneak around them on the playground. I knew I was tired of being called names. Why did they call me "dirty Mexican," anyway? What was that about? I knew Mama always sent me to school clean.

I ran toward the red-headed boy and started swinging my fists and kicking with everything I had in me. I know I got a good swing at his nose, and mine got punched in return. Before I knew it, I was in the middle of a big fight because some of the other boys joined in the fray.

A mob of children had circled as we kicked and punched and swung. Teachers from everywhere came rushing out and started separating us, but I still kicked and punched even as I was being restrained. I could hear the other boys telling their side of the story. When a teacher asked me for an explanation, I didn't know how to answer. I just kept looking down at my feet. I remember my heart was pounding and my body was shaking uncontrollably and, somehow, I managed to keep the tears from flowing.

A teacher grabbed me by the front of my shirt and literally dragged me to the principal's office. I tried to gain my balance and run beside her, but she had very long legs and I couldn't keep up with her. The principal came out from a side room and talked to her briefly. Then he pushed me into his office and shut the door. From behind the door he grabbed a strap and shoved me onto his desk, face down. He pulled down my trousers and smacked me with the strap. I know I must have felt pain as he proceeded to lash at me, but the emotion that would be forever etched in my memory was that of absolute humiliation. In fact, that feeling of humiliation at the memory of that incident haunted me for the rest of my life.

No one else got spanked that day.

That beating was not to be my last, either, because I was slowly beginning to understand what a "dirty Mexican" was, and resentment had its effect on me.

In my young mind the die was cast. I was too young to understand why others chose to treat me with such anger. I was too young to understand the ignorance that caused people to have so much contempt for those who were different or had less. I just knew that it was going to be a fact of my life: that whatever it was they saw in me would be unacceptable to them. And I knew that this was all unacceptable to me.

I was in many more fights on that playground during the time that followed in McFarland. After each fight, I would end up in the principal's office where he would take the strap from behind the door as I clamped my mouth shut. I was determined to not allow him the satisfaction of hearing me cry. He was quite frustrated with this fact and – on one torturous occasion – he exclaimed, "Cry, you little Mexican!"

But I never did.

# 9

## *Tres Mundos / Three Worlds*

I LIVED IN THREE WORLDS. There was the world of my family. There was the world of the playground. There was the world of the classroom.

In the world of my parents, I was a good boy. I was respectful and helped with the many chores. I spoke only Spanish at home and, at my mother's side, learned the *oraciones* – the prayers that would someday get me to Heaven. My parents had no knowledge of what I was enduring at school, because I never shared it with them. Somehow I knew that they wouldn't know how to deal with the trouble I was having. I somehow sensed that they would be intimidated by the principal and the teachers, and so I never let them know about the fights and the principal's ugliness. I had erected a wall between the school and my parents.

On the playground, I became a bad boy. I became a fighter because I wouldn't back down and accept the name-calling and ridicule of the other students. Even though I was light-skinned – with hazel eyes and sandy-brown hair – my worn clothing, broken English, and obvious cultural traits made me a target for the ignorance and hatred of others. Many times my big brothers came to my rescue, as I would go to theirs, and we would often arrive home with bruises and black eyes. Somehow we kept the truth away from our parents.

It seemed that there were two raging dogs fighting within me. One of the dogs was the furious pride I had for my home life and the parents who worked so hard to keep me alive. It seemed to me that my parents were such intelligent and creative people. My father could fix anything, and would tinker with that old Brother and get it humming after we thought it couldn't crawl another mile. There were the fabulous stories he told that I would later learn were classic tales. He seemed to know so much about history and his dramatic renderings would come alive in my imagination. He could conjure poems in his head and he taught us about the constellations: Orion, *El Alacrán,* and the Dippers.

Mama taught me so much about life with her stoic wisdom and her logical explanations. She created the most intricate embroideries – colorful patterns that brought a touch of beauty to our stark surroundings. She would find ways to keep us clothed and *La Segunda*

*Madre* would whir through the evening hours, by lantern light, creating essential clothing from empty flour sacks.

But then the other dog would rear its ugly head. I was beginning to understand the obvious poverty I lived in: the faded clothing, the hand-me-down shoes that were always either too small or too big; the unaccepted language that would earn me a sharp rap on the knuckles if accidentally uttered in school. There were my uneducated parents who could neither read nor write – my father, trying to communicate with the broken English he was slowly acquiring, and my mother signing her name with an "X" for most of her life.

It was with this battle between pride and shame that I wrestled with the world of the classroom. I thank the heavens that I began my first year of education in Miss Miller's classroom. She was very patient with me and very soon I was reading. In later years, I would ponder that great mystery: when and how letters, sounds, and words, all of a sudden made sense. Time seemed to fold over on itself when I, one day, realized that I was speaking English. I didn't notice this transition taking place. My English was broken and hesitant, but it was English.

I viewed Miss Miller as the teacher who held the magic key that unlocked the mystery of reading for me. She seemed genuinely excited when I started to read my first words. Soon I was reading those wonderful books that were stacked in the cupboards. Those books were about children and families and dogs and cats and contained words that read: "This is Jack./ See Jack run./ Run, Jack, run!" Soon I was reading wonderful stories, nursery rhymes, and poems.

However, I always had to be careful to not use the language with which I was most comfortable. If I became excited or wanted to share with another *Mexicano* in the classroom, adrenalin would shoot through me as I realized that a Spanish word had almost slipped out of my mouth. When it would accidentally happen, a teacher would seem to appear out of nowhere – with a wooden ruler or switch – ready to swat my hands or slap the back of my head. It was never a "gentle" reminder.

Over time I started to feel an embarrassment about my home language. I was daily being taught that it was inferior and disgusting. I was just a boy and those who were seemingly more knowing were adamant about beating the language out of me. Yet, this language that was made to seem so ugly was the language that had brought me to this point in my life's journey. It was the language of my mother's gentle reprimands and my father's exciting stories and practical instruction. It was the language of my brothers and sisters as we played and joked and argued and shared our days.

My inquisitive mind noticed that the adults and children in the reading books looked like the teachers and *los gabacho* children at my school. The eye and hair color, the clothing, the houses and cars and furniture, the family celebrations – they all seemed so different than what I experienced in my own life. None of the characters in those books looked like my parents or the *Mexicanos* that lived at the labor camp. Even "Spot" and "Mittens" looked different than the mutts and strays that came to our door for scraps. For a time I felt very confused about this situation, and in my confusion I felt like I was blending into the world of those books. I remember, one day, peering into a mirror trying to catch a glint of blue in my eyes.

# 10

## *La Lucha / The Struggle*

IN THE SUMMER OF 1935, our family moved to a labor camp in Pond, California. Pond was not really a town. It might be described as a gas-station-stop, and the camp was close by. This camp also belonged to Mr. Weller. Another baby was added to the family. Margarita brought gaiety to the family with her joyful smile and twinkling eyes.

Roberto, Francisca, and I were enrolled at Pondham School. The oldest, Manuél, was now working in the fields with our father. The school was located about three miles away from the camp, and there was no school bus to transport us. Every morning, as we'd start on our way, there was a big black German shepherd that would attack and terrorize us. I remember carrying a large stick as we'd tiptoe along the road hoping that he wouldn't spy us. There were times when he'd corner us and bark for what seemed like hours before he tired of the siege and strutted away, tail wagging, triumphant in the knowledge that he made our lives miserable.

Pondham was no different than the school I had left behind. Again I had to deal with the name-calling, as did my brother and sister. We would have to be cautious of our use of Spanish since we had just returned from the long summer months, steeped again in the language of our home life.

The Mexicans and Negros were not allowed to eat in the cafeteria with the other children. We ate under *los olmos,* the elms. During the warm months this situation was fine. Mama supplied us with a lunch that would have brought ridicule from the other children – *tortillas* stuffed with *frijoles*, beans. On rainy days, there we sat – under the dripping branches of the elms – munching our lunch, as large drops of water plopped on our food. On foggy days we would disappear from sight – the misty ground shrouding our bodies as we hurriedly finished our meal so we could return to the playground to run and jump in order to warm our shivering bodies. I could not understand why some children were allowed their meals in the warmth of the cafeteria and others were not. Being a child, I assumed that there had to be a very good reason for such a situation, and so I never questioned.

I loved to read. I think that I did so well in this subject because reading allowed me to disappear into my imagination. The pages of those books whisked me away to far-away lands and long-ago times; stole me away from the meager circumstances of my life. How I wished there were books in our home. I remember seeing a picture at school, in a magazine, of a young boy sitting by a roaring fire reading *The Adventures of Robin Hood.* Behind him was a magnificent bookcase filled with books. I fantasized about entering the picture, snuggling beside him, and reading along.

As I read in school, vivid images would appear in my imagination and I remember my hand twitching and my eyes searching for a pencil and a piece of paper to draw what I saw in my mind's eye. There was no paper or pencil at home, so it was in school that I began my newfound interest in art. Art was my second love and every Friday when art time was squeezed into the day, sheet after sheet of paper became filled with my whimsical creations. I especially became very good at recreating the images of comic book characters. The Phantom, Batman, Pop-Eye, Superman, and Flash Gordon would magically appear upon the white sheets of art paper. The other children in class would circle around me and stare, mesmerized, by my quick and adept renderings. I remember one of my teachers nodding her head in approval as I sketched and shaded.

In 1938 my father was told by Mr. Weller that we would have to move on. Mama packed our few possessions and we moved to Lerdo, California, about thirty miles southeast of Pond, where my father secured a job harvesting sugar beets. We moved into a sorry little house located adjacent to the train tracks and surrounded by uncultivated fields. Actually our house was really just a boxcar that had been abandoned next to the tracks. Mama's kitchen was a lean-to attached to the boxcar. Our house shook every time a train sped by. At night I remember the deafening noise would wake us every few hours and always made us feel like the train would come crashing right through. The younger children would awaken and start screaming, and Mama had quite a time settling them back down. The boxcar was without a heating source and when the weather turned cold, it felt like we were living in an icebox as evidenced by the tiny icicles hanging from the ceiling.

We started at Lerdo School late in the year. The trek to school was truly miserable, especially when the rains came that winter. Again, because there was no bus, we had to walk to school. Though the school was only a few miles away, we had to cross Highway 99 and the railroad tracks. Once we were safely on the other side, we continued our trek toward the school, which was located at the end of a long dirt road. The road was composed of loose dust and dirt that turned into a sea of mud when the rains came. No matter where we stepped, our shoes would become caked and sticky with wet mud. We had no money for shoes that year, and so we wrapped our feet in cardboard and then stuffed our feet into our shoes that were coming apart at the seams. We would then wrap the shoes with twine. By the time we arrived at school we were dripping wet, our shoes sloshing, and water seeping through the holes. We would sit in our classroom with damp clothes, wet shoes, and with our teeth chattering and our bodies shivering.

Mama must have prayed particularly hard during our time in Lerdo, because we maneuvered the busy highway and train tracks without incident and it seems that we were never sick. The women who worked in the cafeteria must have noted our miserable condition, because they recruited us to work in the cafeteria. We would help to serve the lunch meal, and then we would get to sit down and eat after all the children had been served and the tables had been wiped. We devoured that delicious food and basked in the warmth of the cafeteria kitchen.

A kind teacher at the school gave my sister the classroom Christmas tree when the winter break began. We were so excited to have the wilted little tree – our first ever. However, we were somewhat dismayed when the Santa Claus that the other children so deftly described forgot to visit our boxcar home. No matter. Mama erected her treasured *nacimiento* with the tiny Christ Child surrounded with miniature barn animals and shepherds. She made a pot of her delicious *tamales* and led us in singing *canciones de Navidad* on *La Noche de Paz* (Christmas songs on "The Night of Peace" – Christmas Night).

Mr. Weller must have realized that he had lost a good man when he let my father go, because – in the spring of 1939 – he asked my father to return. Mama again brought out the sacks and boxes and we moved back to the labor camp in Pond. To me, that camp was like a little piece of Heaven compared to Lerdo. The reservoir, orchards, and vineyards that surrounded us created a quiet sanctuary and I sensed the peace that came back to my mother's spirit.

I returned to Pondham School in the middle of my seventh grade year. I remember being excited about my studies. The teachers continued to do their jobs because I continued to learn. I continued to learn despite the usual unfairness that seemed to be the regular course of life, both inside and outside of the classroom. I continued to steal away to imaginary places and draw those places when allowed.

That summer, being twelve years old and of working age, I joined my father and brothers in the fields. After the harvest, I returned to school. At the end of the school year, I accomplished an exceptional feat: I graduated from eighth grade. Few children in the latter years of the Depression, especially those whose parents struggled in poverty, attained an eighth grade diploma.

Because my graduating class was so small – with

only twelve graduates – we were to each share something with the audience: a speech, a song, or a talent of some kind. On graduation day, with my parents sitting in the audience, I stood on the stage at Pondham School with an easel and a piece of charcoal in my hand, and speedily drew the whims of the audience. My parents sat amazed, not realizing their son had acquired this talent.

Appearing on the canvasses before me were landscapes, ships at sea, "still life" arrangements, and the ever-popular cartoon characters. The audience rose in applause and I stood there, staring at my hands, and wondering how this magic had come to be.

# 11

## *Invisíble / Invisible*

MANUAL LABOR WAS MY FAMILY'S LEGACY. My father and mother had always worked with their hands in that never-ending struggle to provide for their family. Though my own hands held a talent for art, it was a talent that would have to be temporarily stifled, because I had become "of age" to join my father in the fields. Those artist's hands would now become the rough, calloused hands of a farm worker. It was necessary that I join my father and brothers in the fields, at least in the summer months, weekends, and during the harvest, in order to help provide for the family. And it seems that no matter how hard we worked, we continued to live with the bare essentials and could seldom afford even the smallest luxuries.

After the harvest of 1940, my brother Manuél

continued to work with my father, and Roberto and I were allowed to return to school. At 5:30 in the morning we would catch the school bus to Delano High School. The high school was located in the town of Delano, which was six miles from the labor camp in Pond. Though we started a month and a half late, we quickly acclimated ourselves to the new school. One of my first impressions, as I started my freshman year, was to recognize how shoddy and "old fashioned" my shoes and clothes were. As a child I was aware of this situation, but had never been too bothered by it.

Now, as an adolescent, the shocking reality was more apparent. Many of the boys on campus were wearing the latest styles: Levi pants, Woodsmen buckled boots, and watch fobs. I was embarrassed by my clothing, but didn't dare ask my parents for new, more modern clothes because I knew there was no money for such things. I should feel grateful that my father bought me a new pair of pants and some canvas shoes to start back to school. However, why my father decided to buy me a pair of bright green pants, I'll never know. But I do know that I walked through the halls of that school with my eyes downcast, wanting to disappear into the walls. I remember thinking how good it would be to be invisible. Then it occurred to me that, in the eyes of many at that school, I was already invisible.

One day, during lunch break, a group of us Mexican boys were huddled together sharing our *chistes,* jokes.

Teasing among ourselves, we spoke the language of our parents – the language with which we were most comfortable and could best express our thoughts and feelings. We were always careful to keep our talking low and to ourselves. I was now very aware of the fact that school life was segregated. We *Mexicanos* were never actually told to stay with others of our own kind, but there was always an uneasy tension and an unspoken rule that we were not to mix with *los gabachos*.

As we talked and laughed, a teacher walked by. I noticed, out of the corner of my eye, that she walked a few steps away, stopped, turned, and came back to our group. She stood there, arms crossed, glaring angrily at us. It took our little group a few moments to recognize her presence and quiet down. She continued to stare with an impatient scowl on her face until there was an uncomfortable silence. And then she said, slowly and measured, "How dare you speak that *barbaric* language in this school!"

She then turned on her heels and marched away, shaking her head, disgusted.

We boys just stood there. I don't know what the others were thinking, but I was fighting within myself; shame and rage were mingling and brewing. As I looked at my friends, I noticed that they all stood there with their heads down, shoulders stooped – one shuffling his foot on the ground. Then, as if on cue, we just walked away in different directions and disappeared into the hubbub of the quad.

I would give much thought to the problems that I was encountering in school and in the outside world because of the fact that I was a *Mexicano*, and to the anxious feelings that those problems were stirring within me. For instance, as a child I never thought twice about the fact that, when attending the cinema, we *Mexicanos* were never allowed to sit in the main hall of the theater. We would be ferried, along with the Chinese, Japanese, Negroes, and Filipinos, to the balcony. As an adolescent, this reality started to bother me. Although I would attend the cinema, eager to sit engrossed with the comedy or drama before me, I was always fighting within myself. Why did I automatically climb to the balcony without being told? I knew that *así es porque así es.* But why were things "such"? Could they be changed? If not . . . why not? Why did this situation make me feel that I was less of a human being? Why did some feel a need to keep me "in my place?"

All these questions whirled around in my head and heart, but there were no answers. There was just frustration and shame.

My best memory of Delano High School was art class and the wonderful teacher who made the world of color, shapes, and line come alive. Miss Claire Hoster immediately acknowledged my talent and began to teach me the fundamentals of art and design. Prior to coming to her class, my artistic endeavors were totally self-directed, but under her guidance I was learning the hidden secrets of perspective, form, line, and color. It was in art class that I felt some sense of worth. I felt unique. My heart would swell with pride when she addressed me as "Diego Rivera," the great Mexican muralist whom I didn't even know existed until I came to Miss Hoster's classroom.

In 1941, three months after I started at Delano High, my family was forced to move from the Weller ranch. So, I left Miss Hoster and my *amigos* – my friends in Delano and at the labor camp – and moved with my family into a small house at 846 "D" Street in the outskirts of Wasco, California, some twenty miles north of Pond. This house was like a palace compared to the houses at the camp. It had an indoor tub, a flushing toilet, and a gas stove.

Roberto attended Wasco High School for a short time and then decided to join my father and brother Manuél in the orchards and vineyards surrounding Wasco. I would walk to the school which was located on the other side of town but, since Wasco was a small town, the walk was not too bad. I was still a freshman and, of course, starting very late into the school year. Luckily, I entered the classrooms of two teachers who were going to make an impact on my life in a good way.

Every day after school, Miss Casey, my English teacher, would give me extra tutoring with pronunciation. She seemed to take a liking to me and told me that she thought – with a little help – I could lose some of my accent and learn to better pronounce my words. Again I began to feel self-conscious about my parents' language, but then she said something that seemed unbelievable. I even wondered if I had really heard her say: "Spanish is a very ancient language, Alfonso. It is beautiful. Never lose it."

Those few words threw me into a stir of confusion. I had never heard a teacher say such a thing. I wanted to believe her words, but my young mind could not process their truth. Though I tried to believe those words, it would take years before I could be free from the shame that had been instilled in me concerning the language that I loved.

Curiously, after Miss Casey's remark, I began to get very excited about perfecting my English. She would never know how those simple words had affected my attitude about learning. Those simple words had fanned a tiny ember of self-worth.

Miss Casey worked so hard to get my mouth to correctly pronounce certain words, especially those that contained the "sh" sound. Over and over again, I was made to pronounce "ship" and "sheet" which I pronounced as "chip" and "cheet."

She also pointed out the English words that had Spanish imbedded in them. She told me that Spanish had come from the language of the great Romans – Latin. My understanding of vocabulary seemed to soar as I found those familiar parts hidden in so many words. Why she spent so much time with me, I'll never know. But she did, and gradually my confidence grew and I would read outloud to myself. I became aware of my diction and continued to feel excited about my newfound ability.

Mr. Hauss was very impressed with my artistic talent. One day he invited the seventh and eighth graders from the grammar school to a "demonstration" of my skills. A line was formed that flowed out of the art room. One by one, children entered and made their requests as my hand stealthily sketched and shaded across the paper at the easel. I signed my name, "Al Espinosa," at the bottom of each sample. As I completed each sketch, the children started to gather in groups, excitedly comparing their sheets with others. Farm scenes, animals like dogs and horses, landscapes, comic book heroes and spaceships, flowed from my imagination onto the blank canvasses. My hand and arm would start to cramp, but my mind was alive with energy as I was transported to another world – a world that did not judge me by my worn clothing or the accent in my words.

Mr. Hauss instructed me to stay after class one day and asked if I would consider doing a comic strip for the high school newspaper. I remember thinking that this was an impossible thing, since I had never seen a Mexican surname on any of the articles in the paper.

"Well, think about it, Alfonso. I think you'd do a good job," he offered as he turned and walked back to his desk. "By the way," he added, turning and looking directly into my eyes, "the city newspaper is interested in your work."

On my way home that day I didn't even remember the trek across town. I was too excited, with all kinds of emotions jumbled and jumping within me. As I approached the house, I noticed my father's pickup under the mulberry tree. I was surprised that he was home so early. When I entered the house, my father was leaning on the gas stove talking to my mother. My words of good news were ready to tumble out of my mouth when I caught some of my father's words – *"ya vamos . . . los muchachos . . . trabajar . . . pa' Santa Maria."* Those few words caused my heart to sink. He was telling my mother that he would be leaving Wasco. He would be taking my brothers and me to work in the fields in the vicinity of Santa Maria, a hundred miles away to the west. We would be leaving as soon as possible. I didn't dare protest, nor did I dare share with my parents the wonderful opportunity that Mr. Hauss had presented to me that day.

My father, brothers, and I worked hard in the fields near Santa Maria that spring and summer and into the fall. In the spring, rain would pour down on us as we toiled in the mud. Rainbows would then appear as did the wildflowers on the surrounding hills and I pined for a box of watercolors to record the beauty amidst the drudgery of the work. In the summer, we worked under the glaring rays of the sun, stooped close to the ground with short-handled hoes, heaving away at tangled roots. Sometimes cool ocean breezes would sweep down into the valley and we'd stand, stretch, and bask in the refreshing *brisas*.

We lived in a tent at a labor camp and since Mama had stayed in Wasco with my younger siblings, we men had to fend for ourselves. We ate a lot of canned beans and store-bought bread. We worked from sunup to sundown, seven days a week, and sent most of our pay back to the family. We didn't just stay for the beet thinning, but found other jobs and then stayed into September and October for the harvest of various crops.

In the fall of 1941, we returned to Wasco and I started back at Wasco High School as a sophomore, several months late as usual. The excitement with which I left Wasco would not greet me when I returned. The whole world had taken on an ominous pallor and so had my own life.

# 12

## *La Guerra / The War!*

STARTING LATE INTO THE SCHOOL YEAR was a recurring situation that was starting to do its damage on my attitude. School was hard enough without the aggravation and embarrassment of starting late, having to catch up, and feeling scrutinized each time I entered a new classroom.

The admit slip indicated that Miss Main was my English teacher. I was somewhat excited about this class because I was feeling confident with my reading abilities. However, when I entered her class on that first day, I had a strange sensation. First of all, I noticed that most of the students were *gabachos*; there was no scattered mixing of minorities that made up the usual classroom. I hadn't realized it at the time, and I would only learn later, that my freshman English teacher, Miss Casey, had given me an "A." Leaving Wasco in such a rush, my report card was misplaced during the long time that I was gone, and I had no knowledge that I had received my first "excellent" grade in English. Because of this high mark, and with Miss Casey's recommendation, I had been placed in an advanced English class.

When I handed my admit slip to Miss Main, she stared at it incredulously. *There seems to be a serious mistake* was the thought that seemed to be plastered on her face. She pointed to a desk. In my new-boy timidity, it seemed that all eyes in the classroom glared contemptuously at me. As I made my way to the desk, I became very aware of my high-water trousers, my sun-bleached shirt, and my dirt-stained shoes. There was a distinct line on my forehead – the top part was my natural skin tone and the bottom sunburned brown where the rim of my work hat had left its impression. I sat down feeling conspicuous and out-of-place. Because I had, up to that point, no knowledge of my previous grade, I felt certain that there had, indeed, been a mistake in my placement. However, as the class continued, I began to feel at ease. I started to relax when I heard my classmates read, one at a time, as Miss Main directed the round-robin reading. Not only did I surmise that I could read as well as they could, the class was reading a book entitled *A Tale of Two Cities* that I had read before and had enjoyed.

Although I had no book in front of me, I became

entranced with the story as classmates took their turns reading and my imagination took hold. It didn't occur to me that I should have a book, instead I was preoccupied with the newness of the class, the unsettling emotions and the beauty of the prose. Suddenly I heard my name called and I was yanked from my absorption.

"Alfonso, read!"

Miss Main's impatient command came crisp and precise.

I immediately realized that I had no book and looked around in confusion. Miss Main did not offer to hand me a book. Instead, she walked toward me with her pointer and poked it into my chest several times.

"Read!" she commanded again, knowing full well that I had no book, jabbing at me again and then lifting the pointer as if she wanted to strike me with it. I felt my face flush with embarrassment and with anger. I wanted to grab the pointer and break it in two. A student next to me pointed under my chair. I looked and there was a book on the floor. I picked up the book and started leafing through the pages. Miss Main made no offer to tell me the page number. The same sympathetic student whispered the page number to me. I glanced up into Miss Main's face as she glared at that student with a look of *this is not your business.*

I fidgeted for a moment and then found the page. I quickly skimmed the page to find the starting place. I took a deep breath and began to read.

"Stand up!" she growled, interrupting my feeble start.

I looked around the room trying to remember if the other students had been made to stand while they read. Because I had become so mesmerized with the story, I honestly could not remember if they had stood while reading. Something in my gut told me that I was being made an exception and that Miss Main was intent on showcasing my obvious ignorance to the rest of the class.

I stood.

I took another deep breath and began to read.

The tense atmosphere started to ease as the students realized that I was an able reader. *Perhaps Miss Main is satisfied and will leave the "new kid" alone*, seemed to be their attitude as they began to relax into their seats. At a break in the story I looked up and noticed that Miss Main was slowly nodding her head in approval, however, her features were still hard and she still seemed perturbed. Feeling energized with my progress, I proceeded until I suddenly came to a word that I was not sure how to pronounce.

The word before me was "admiral." I paused and looked intently at the word. I could hear my heart pounding in my ears as I silently tried to form the syllables into something that sounded familiar. I said it in my head in Spanish, and then, in English, I blurted out something that sounded like *ad-mire-rawl.*

"What did you say?" Miss Main's immediate response came out of her mouth like pellets falling out of a gun.

I hesitated for half a second, wondering if she really hadn't heard me.

"*Ad . . .mire . . .rawl.*" The word crawled out of my mouth like sticky syrup being coaxed from a jar.

Several of the students burst out laughing, having held their giggles at my first attempt. I felt like running out of the classroom, but I knew that that would only add to my embarrassment. I stood there facing Miss Main, forcing myself to stand straight, feeling my face involuntarily twitching. The outburst quickly subsided as the class registered the menacing look on Miss Main's face. The classroom became deathly quiet and I thought that perhaps Miss Main was ready to reprimand the students for their rudeness.

Instead, looking steadily into my eyes, she said, "Don't you know anything, you stupid Mexican?"

Again, a few nervous giggles sprinkled throughout the classroom.

I continued to look into Miss Main's arrogant eyes as she glared back, unblinking. I closed the open book. I filled my lungs with a steady inhale and then threw that book with all my strength across the classroom. Miss Main jerked at the sound of that book smashing against the blackboard and then falling to the floor. The room again became eerily quiet. I held my gaze into her eyes but, surprisingly, felt drained of emotion. I just felt empty. And then I walked out of the classroom.

I received an "F" in English that semester because I refused to go back to Miss Main's class and the school refused to assign me to a different teacher.

On December 7, 1941, the Japanese attacked Pearl Harbor. All the students at Wasco High were assembled in the auditorium as the principal announced that our country was officially in a state of war. That evening, huddled around our radio, we heard the voice of President Roosevelt declare war on Japan, Germany, and Italy. The newsreels that we had viewed at the cinema, reporting the atrocities that were happening overseas, heralded that "day of infamy" that would affect my life adversely and cause more hardship for my family.

The following month, a new child was added to the family. My baby sister, Belen, was born on January 26, 1942, and in June of that year, my eldest brother, Manuel, was inducted into the army. I remember the panic in my mother's eyes at hearing the news that her son would be shipped overseas. I also saw the disappointment in her eyes when my father announced that we would be leaving Wasco.

# 13

## *Diego Rivera*

I WAS VERY TIRED of the constant moving. I knew that it could not be helped – that my father found work where he could. We moved to a labor camp near Richgrove, California. The camp was named *El Rancho California* and was located about eighteen miles northeast of Wasco. Leaving our "little palace" in Wasco and coming to this primitive camp was disheartening. Again, my mother would be sweeping dirt floors and we would be using outside latrines. The walls of our shack were constructed of wooden slats with obvious separations that allowed the wind and dust to flow freely through the house. That winter was particularly cold with frost ruining the citrus crops. Again, we lived in a virtual icebox and fierce blasts of frigid air threatened to bring the house down.

The house was actually too small for our large family, now numbering ten, so we older boys slept in a tent outside of the house. I remember coming out of the tent in the mornings, my hands and feet numb, and looking up at the Sierra Nevada Mountains that loomed above the camp. The mountains were breathtakingly beautiful, with pristine snow draping the summits, and I wondered how something so beautiful could cause so much misery – those majestic pavilions sending frozen winds to whip down upon our family.

I would catch the school bus to Delano High. Most of my old friends were no longer in school. Many *Mexicanos* dropped out of school to work the fields. Because so many young men were leaving the area to join the armed forces, those of us who were left would have to fill the labor void. My family sorely missed the contribution that Manuel had made to the family's sustenance. And then my brother Robert left to join the Marines.

I continued on at Delano High, grateful that my father did not insist that I join him in the fields, but feeling disheartened, lonely for my brothers, and eager to be of age to join them on the battlefields. Because of the "F" I had received at Wasco High School, I was again placed in lower classes. I was bored and felt unchallenged and I began to believe that, no matter how I tried, I would never be able to rise above my low status. I thought about the great power that teachers had for good or evil – with the stroke of a pen, with a casual remark, they could change a person's life forever. At times, I felt that I had no business believing that I would be anything but a manual laborer. Feelings of invisibility again plagued me as I walked the halls of Delano High.

One day I heard a familiar voice shout from across the quad.

"Diego!"

At first I did not respond because, of course, that was not my name. However, Miss Hoster's voice was distinct and I immediately remembered the moniker she used in art class the previous year.

"Diego . . . Alfonso, you're back!" she exclaimed enthusiastically and with her welcoming smile. She wore the familiar smock, splattered with paint, that I thought one day might be worth a lot of money if stretched across a frame and sold as art.

"Yes, Miss Hoster!" I responded, surprised that she had remembered me.

"Al, I've been thinking about you . . . and a project that I have in mind. Walk with me and I'll explain it to you."

We walked across the quad as she described, with flamboyant waves of her hands, the giant mural that she imagined being painted on the outside wall of the school auditorium. As she spoke, my heart began to pound and I became giddy with excitement at the possibility of working on such a project.

I would go to her classroom at lunchtime and together we would peruse magazines and art history books detailing the media and techniques used by the Mexican mural painters. I felt as if my heart would burst when I saw the majestic creations of Diego Rivera, Siqueiros, and Orozco. Not only was I mesmerized by the colors and forms used by the great muralists, I was intrigued by the social messages they translated onto walls for all to see. Color and form seemed to burst out of the two-dimensional surfaces to scream out the defiant message of "Enough!"

As I worked with Miss Hoster in the art room, I felt like I was in my second home. The room was a happy mess with student art on the walls and canvasses drooping sloppily from cupboards. Rulers, planes, and brushes of varying sizes protruded from rusty coffee cans and empty mayonnaise jars. Paint was splattered like confetti on the walls, floor, and table-tops. I inhaled the scent of oils, pastels, inks, clays, and solvents. Those aromas had always stirred excitement within me and took my reverie back to that very first day of school when those aromatic sensations had helped to turn my fear into anticipation.

Miss Hoster and I worked for several weeks designing a mural that would exhibit the Delano High School mascot. We designed a ferocious tiger that seemed to be pouncing out of the wall. I was so excited about the project that I often went without eating. I had to work during lunch because it would be a very long walk home if I missed the bus at the end of the school day.

I also didn't eat because, for some reason, I had no appetite. My mother noticed that I didn't eat much at breakfast nor at dinner. The once unsatisfied hunger pangs of a growing boy just seemed to diminish.

"*Cóme, mi hijíto,*" she would beg. "Please eat," and I would take a few more bites, forcing the food down.

One afternoon, while out running the track during P.E., I was unable to finish the assigned distance. I stopped and almost fell to the ground, faint and exhausted. Mr. Daniels, my football coach, came over to me and placed his hand on my drooping head. Then he traced his fingers over the bony protrusion of my shoulder blade.

"Al, have you been to a doctor?" he asked with a concerned look in his eyes. "Have you ever been tested for tuberculosis?"

I shook my head in the negative and wondered why he would ask such a question.

Mr. Daniels looked at me gravely, then walked away, but his words stayed on my mind.

I knew that something wasn't right with me. It was becoming increasingly hard for me to get out of bed in the mornings. Some nights I felt that I was going to freeze. I would start shivering and couldn't stop even after Mama put extra blankets on me. I slept in my coat and shoes, but still the shivers would come and then I would start to cough. The chills and coughing kept me awake throughout the night. When morning came, I was exhausted.

But the mural awaited me. I would muster my strength to get out of bed and to the bus before it rumbled off and left me behind. I tried to ignore the fact that as I dressed for school I could double my belt around my waist and that I had to stuff handkerchiefs under my shirt to try to look less bony.

My father was now the sole support of our family. Though Manuel and Robert sent home portions of their military pay, we were living hand-to-mouth. One evening I overheard my parents talking about our dire situation. There were nine of us now living in that hovel and my father was starting to slow down even though he managed to find steady work. Though I was feeling physically weak and wanted so much to continue my education, I knew that I had to make a decision.

The next morning, I dragged myself out of the tent earlier than usual. I washed and dressed and walked into the kitchen as my father took his last sip of coffee. Without a word, he got up from the table and went out the door into the early morning darkness. I followed him.

I was sixteen years old.

The tiger mural was never completed.

The "Diego Rivera" of Delano High did not return

to school.

# PART THREE

# 14

## *Ilusiónes / Illusions*

I HAD MY GOOD DAYS and my bad days.

The struggle to get out of bed in the mornings continued to plague me, but somehow I managed, and began to learn new skills at my father's side. I was taught how to drive and was put in charge of driving *La Huevona,* our rickety work truck, to and from the fields with a truckload of workers. Sometimes the tires would bounce a little too violently over the potholes and sometimes I'd make a curve much too quickly and my passengers would almost be tossed out and then they'd curse and shake their fists at me. But they didn't complain too much because I always seemed to get them to the fields on time, ready to start work when *los jefes* arrived. I also got very good at tying vines, girdling and picking grapes. Because I closely watched my father work the irrigation pipes, seeing how he guided the water and carefully calculated the speed and amount of water, I aspired to one day be an expert irrigator.

New houses were built at the California Ranch. They were constructed out of cement block and had four rooms – including a bathroom with an in-door flushing toilet and a shower stall. Incredibly, these houses had glass windows. They also had swamp coolers that would blow noisy drafts of air throughout the house on hot summer days. However, in the winter, the cement blocks seemed to soak in the freezing temperatures and didn't allow the moisture to escape and sometimes the walls would start to get moldy. Mama, Francisca and Alícia would scrub at the walls to get the mold off.

Our house had a front porch and I remember coming home from work on spring and summer days to see Mom on the porch, in the shade, as my younger siblings played in the yard. She'd sit peacefully, her rosary beads dangling from her fingers, and I knew that she was praying that the angels and *La Virgen de Guadalupe* would keep close watch over Manuel and Robert. She seemed happy and planted colorful flowers of several varieties, including her beloved periwinkles, all around the outside perimeter of the house and in the yard. Dad planted a garden of vegetables and berries.

We had lots of neighbors at the camp, including *braceros*. *Braceros* were young men from Mexico who had been recruited to work in the fields, especially during the harvest, in the absence of the many men who had gone off to war. Although these *braceros* – these men that "worked with their arms" – carried few possessions, there was always a guitar or two among them. On cool evenings we *vecinos,* young and old, would gather around a blazing open fire, fed by crackling grape or almond stumps. We would sing beloved *rancheras,* the Mexican country songs. I, too, learned to play the guitar and found that I had quite a singing voice. We'd strum at our *guitarras,* sing, shout *gritos,* laugh and carouse. These festive reprieves seemed to ease the drudgery of the long workdays.

It was during one of these evenings that I met Consuelo. Actually, I had often seen "Connie" around the camp playing with her sisters or helping her mother with the laundry. One evening I looked across the roaring bond fire and noticed a most beautiful young lady. It was Connie, looking all grown-up, and she glanced back at me shyly. I had never talked much to girls, except my own sisters, and decided I'd talk to her and pretend that I was talking to one of my sisters. The strategy worked because we were soon talking and joking with each other and, in awhile, we were considered *novios* – "boyfriend and girlfriend." We'd walk together into the vineyards that surrounded the labor camp, holding hands and clumsily experimenting with kissing. We never got too far, because Connie's mom and the other women at the camp kept an eye on all of us youngsters.

Connie was a sweetheart and I really liked her. Some of the young people at the camp were already talking about marriage. She asked me if I'd like to marry her and I remember getting really nervous. There were so many things that I wanted to do with my life. For sure, I wanted to go off to war. Maybe, someday, I would go back to school. And besides, I was only seventeen. But I was sweet on Connie so I didn't say *no* – but I didn't say *yes* either.

On Fridays, after a long workweek, my dad would travel into Delano to visit the Federal Price Administration. This agency had been set up during the war to distribute stamps that could then be used to purchase gasoline and some items that were being rationed because of the war. Without these stamps it was impossible to purchase certain items. One day he invited me to accompany him. When we entered the building, I noticed that one of the lines was quite a bit longer than the others. I followed my father who seemed to know by instinct what line to get into although all the lines had identical signs above them. Soon I realized why this particular line was so long. At the window of this particular line, stood an attractive young lady who spoke Spanish! Sure enough, most of the people in that line were *Mexicanos* and they got into her line because she was able to help them using her fluent and flowing Spanish.

As we moved closer to her window, I immediately recognized her.

I remembered a warm summer afternoon some time before my brother Robert left for the military. I was on the ground unfastening my bicycle wheel, dreading the trek into town to have it repaired. I looked up between the spokes and saw my brother approach with two of the most beautiful women I had ever seen. The taller of the two came toward me and stood beside the bike. She smiled down at me. She seemed so tall and she was slim and dressed very stylishly. The red lipstick on her lips glistened, and her teeth – they were so white! I felt petrified. I started to fumble around, attempting to unbolt the bicycle wheel, trying to busy my hands so that I might stop shaking.

"Al," my brother awkwardly offered, "meet Mary and Josephine."

"Mary, Josie," he went on, "this is my kid brother, Al." My brother sounded so formal and proper, it took everything I had in me to not burst out laughing. And I would have if I hadn't felt so darn goofy myself.

I stood up and dusted off my baggy, high-water pants. There was grease smudged on my face and dirt in my hair. I could feel beads of sweat coursing down my forehead and down my back. I extended my greasy hand to Mary.

Her smile!

I was in love.

And then I imagined how I must look and smell. Instinctively, I wanted to smell under my arm but, luckily, I resisted the temptation. I felt my face burn and could imagine the bright red color that flushed my ears and cheeks. I was probably the same shade as her lipstick!

Mary gave me a hearty handshake.

"Good to meet you . . . Al?"

"Yes. It's Alfonso. But, yes, call me Al or Alfonso, or Al . . . yeah, Al's fine or," I shrugged, "Alfonso . . . I guess." I felt like my mouth was full of cotton and I was running it off like an idiot.

"Al," she said again with a smile. Then she and Josephine walked away and I got back to my task, but not really, because I kept peeking over to where she stood with Robert. I felt so darn young and stupid – just a stuttering fool! She seemed so smart and sophisticated.

I was to learn later that Mary Zaragoza was newly graduated from high school, with straight "A's" and had excelled in her business classes. Though she was a *Mexicana* she had been hired right out of high school by the U.S. government to work at the Federal Price Administration. She was the first *Mexicana* to get a professional job on Main Street in Delano. It was to her line at the FPA that all the *Mexicanos* flocked.

When my father and I got up to her window, she

graciously acknowledged my father.

"*Señor Espinosa! Cómo estás? Cómo puedo ayudarte?*" ("Mr. Espinosa! How are you? How can I help you?") Her words flowed smoothly from her beautiful mouth, but before my father could respond, she turned her head to me and nodded.

"Hi, Al. Good to see you again." Her greeting was warm and genuine. I couldn't believe that she actually remembered me! But just as suddenly as my excitement ignited, I felt a rush of embarrassment come over me. Again, those old enemies, shame and self-deprecation, paid their visit. I was just a poor, skinny high school drop-out from the labor camp. Mary was way out of my league.

My father finished his transaction and with an "*adiós*" we walked out together. I turned to get one last glance at Mary and she was already busily at work, helping the next in line.

# 15

## *La Locura / The Madness*

MY FATHER WAS A GOOD FATHER, but a hard father. Working beside him in the fields helped to cement the respect that I had always had for him. I witnessed the respect that others had for him, too. He always seemed to get the jobs with the most prestige as a foreman or supervisor. The farmers we worked for sought him out and knew him by name. It seemed to me that my father knew all there was to know about farming and could fix any problem that arose whether mechanical or social. The workers always came to him with their concerns and he could then take these issues to the farmers. With his broken English, he would act as a mediator.

However, my father was not the easiest person to get along with. I was opinionated and always had so much to say about my thoughts – always thinking about things.

We'd get into arguments and, though I felt I had some very good and logical views, his stubborn insistence would always win out. Once he decided on a matter it was almost impossible to convince him otherwise.

We never talked about my decision to leave school. Although there was an ache in my heart about this decision, I never shared those feelings with my father. It's not that I believed my father didn't care. We had an unspoken understanding that there really wasn't a choice – our family would have suffered if I hadn't joined him in the fields. Perhaps his pride was hurt that he could not provide for the family on his own, but after I left school, I sensed a coldness come over my father.

In his stubbornness, my father refused to acknowledge that I was sick. When I would try to talk to him about how weak I was feeling, he would overpower me with his gruff voice. Sometimes he'd just start telling me that I was crazy to believe I was sick. He'd tell me I looked fine, that this sickness was in my imagination and that I was just giving in to self-pity. I could, sometimes, understand his attitude because I knew what a hard life my father had lived and I had never heard him complain. He was an optimist who knew that somehow he and his family would survive all the ugliness that life threw at us.

I remembered one late evening, the old pickup coming to a stop in front of the house and my father getting out and approaching the house whistling a tune.

I knew he must have been very tired but that whistle gave me reassurance. I believed that all the heartache and dilemmas our family encountered would turn out okay as long as I kept hearing that whistle.

Sometimes he'd get very angry with me and accuse me of exaggerating my symptoms. I sensed the fear in my father's behavior toward my obvious decline. I fought a sickening sensation in my belly when I allowed myself to admit that my father didn't have any idea how to deal with my illness.

I, too, wrestled with the possibility that I was really sick and – when fear would seep into my heart – I'd plug those holes with all kinds of excuses for why I was not healthy. I would tell myself that because I was so young, this was a temporary ailment and that I'd soon recover. My father's obstinate attitude seemed to be a panacea for me and I would talk myself out of accepting my steady worsening because, after all, *"Padre sabe todo"* – "Papa knows everything."

But, during my eighteenth year, several things happened that caused me to realize that we were both fooling ourselves.

When I turned eighteen, I hitched a ride and traveled thirty miles north to Tulare, California, to see a navy recruiter. Manuel was in the army, Robert was a Marine, and it was my plan to join the navy. I was filled with so much anticipation that my insides would turn with excitement as I contemplated all the places I would see as a sailor. I knew that, if given the chance, I would surely bring home a medal for bravery. I'd imagine myself standing tall and handsome in my uniform, with Connie at my arm all proud and sassy. I calculated that my salary, along with my brothers' pay, would surely help keep the family going.

There were other young men in the recruiting office that afternoon when I arrived. I remember squelching all kinds of negative thoughts as I became uncomfortably aware that those other boys looked more robust and muscular compared to me. My name was called and I walked into a white, sun-lit room that was empty, except for a single table with two officers sitting behind it. I stood before them with my arms at my sides. The two officers stared at me in silence. I stretched my head up higher and tried to puff my chest out, but could imagine how pathetic I must have looked. One of the officers cleared his throat and said, "Son, we'll send you into the exam room but . . . have you already seen a doctor?"

Those words caused my heart to race because I could hear Mr. Daniel's ominous words echoing in my memory from that day I collapsed in high school.

A quick exam confirmed that I was not qualified for military duty.

"You need medical attention, and you need it now," were the succinct words of the doctor who examined me.

A dejection I could not put into words overcame me.

Frustration made me want to curse the heavens. Fear made me want to beg the heavens for mercy. Those two emotions put me into the grip of anxiety as I rode a bus back to Delano. I then walked the eight miles back to the California Ranch; all the way cursing, praying, sobbing, shouting, begging, then cursing some more.

I arrived late in the evening and walked into the dimly-lit kitchen and found my dad at the table, his head in his hands.

*"Estoy enfermo, Papa . . .* I'm sick," were the words that fell from my mouth.

He sat there immobile, not even acknowledging my presence. He didn't say a word to me.


My father refused to speak to me for a long time after that evening. Only necessary grunts and curt commands came my way. I continued to get up in the mornings and go to work. I lived in a kind of nightmare, not knowing what to do. I had never been to a doctor in my life and I certainly didn't have the money to pay for one. I didn't know of any place I could go to get help.

My cough was becoming increasingly worse. The alkali and sulfur that were sprayed onto the grapevines and orchards were irritating my lungs as never before. One early morning I was in a row of grapevines, tying the vines and clipping unnecessary shoots, when I started to cough. I had been coughing up blood for some time, but on this day my cough seemed to send a forked tool into my lungs, ripping and tearing, and blood started to come out of my mouth in bright red clumps. The pain was so searing that I fell to the ground clutching my chest and throat. Blood was splattered on my shirt and mucous-filled blood was smeared on my hands. It seems that I lay there for a long time on the cold ground until the coughing subsided. I got myself up and walked out of the row. I was weak from the hemorrhaging and I remember walking with unsteady steps as workers took notice of my appearance and shouted anxiously for my father.

My father appeared out of nowhere, and came up to me and guided me toward the truck. We got into the truck and got to the house where I fell into bed and Mom came into the room, looking panicked and wiping the blood and perspiration from my mouth, chest, and hands.

I slept for the rest of the day and, in the evening, I awoke to find a strange man hovering over me. There was a candle flickering on the bed stand and this man was shaking a strange object over the length of my body. This object looked like a ball of feathers. It made a rattling noise. There was a heavy rancid aroma in the room. I didn't recognize the language I was hearing. It wasn't English. It wasn't Spanish.

I was to learn later that this man was a *curandero*, a kind of folk doctor, who lived in Richgrove. It was said that he had healing powers, so my father sought him out and brought him back to the camp. As the curandero chanted his curious words, I felt my eyes become heavy with fatigue and I fell back into a deep, dreamless sleep.

The next morning I awoke to a quiet house, the cacophony of noises that usually greeted my Saturday sleep was hushed. Mom came into my room, smiled her sad smile, and asked me how I was feeling. She sat at my bed and stroked my forehead with her soothing hands. I felt weak but rested. As we talked, I realized that I had actually been asleep for three days. Mom told me that I had struggled with a high fever and had finally come out of it.

I didn't return to work for several days and then decided I would get myself up and back to my usual routine. My legs, however, felt like they were caked in dried cement, and I had no appetite. Mom fed me *caldos*, soups made from chicken and beef stock, and this seemed to be the only thing my nauseated stomach could allow.

I knew I was still very sick.

My father approached me one day with an excited expression on his face. He went on to tell me that he secured the name of a doctor in Hanford, California, a Doctor Johnston, who many *Mexicanos* were seeing. This doctor seemed to have the cure for all kinds of illnesses.

The next day we got into my dad's pickup and made the fifty-mile trip to Hanford. I remember the bumpy ride down the roads that cut through the seemingly endless rows of grapevines, orchards, and fields of corn, cotton, and potatoes. We got onto Highway 99, traveling north, and in a few hours we arrived at the office of Dr. Johnston.

After an exam, the doctor told me to translate his prognosis to my father. Although my father had acquired a working proficiency in English, the doctor addressed me and insisted that I translate his words into Spanish.

He directed me to tell my father that I could be cured, but that I had to follow his instructions for vitamins and special herbs carefully and strictly. As I translated, my spirits started to perk up. Good health seemed to be in my immediate future! However, the doctor's special vitamins would be expensive and we'd have to make regular visits back to his office.

As I translated, I noted that my father's face had a hard expression. I knew he was mentally calculating the cost, time, and commitment that the doctor's words were suggesting.

We left Dr. Johnston's office with a shake of hands and my father and I drove home in silence. I held a bag of concoctions in my lap and felt confident that I held a miracle cure in my arms.

The following week we returned to Dr. Johnston. And we returned the next week after that. This routine continued for many weeks at great cost in time and money. I was feeling increasingly guilty about the financial strain I was putting on the family and I was getting no better.

I started to deal with fevers that would come over me suddenly, and the wrenching coughs that continued to seize my body. It seems that my health declined along with my will to get well. I started to have nightmares, tossing and turning in a sweat, seeing myself in a coffin being lowered into the ground. I would wake up with a start, my heart racing, perspiration dripping from my face. Then the coughing would begin again and I wanted to scream in anguish and surrender.

There were moments when I just wanted to give up, disgusted with the whole tired mess of my life. Then fear would grip me. I did not want to die. I had so much life to live – so much life ahead of me. I wanted to see the world. I wanted to marry Connie. If only I could wake up one morning and be well. *If only.* I would then give in to tears because I felt so helpless.

One hot summer morning, I could not get out of bed. It felt like a vice had tightened around my chest and I could barely breathe. The sheets of my bed were soaked in sweat. I was so feverish and uncomfortable that I tossed the sheets off my body. The air was so stagnant that this action seemed to make little difference. My sheet-white legs had usually been concealed by trousers during the day and covered by blankets at night. When I tossed the sheets off that morning and drew my legs up,

I glanced down and stared, horrified, at the sight before me. I saw loose, pale skin hanging from the bones of my calves and thighs. My kneecaps protruded like baseballs.

At the sight of my legs, I started to sob and then the coughing set in, and a great wad of blood and mucous was ejected from my throat onto the sheets. I lay there in sweat and blood, my skeletal legs shaking as my body convulsed.

I turned my head toward the bedroom door and saw my father standing there.

He had a strange expression on his face. He, too, was riveted to the terrifying sight of my skeletal legs. I believe, at that moment, it finally struck him as to how sick I really was. His eyes seemed to be filled with panic and helplessness. A nervous sound came out of his mouth sounding oddly like a stifled laugh. I stared back at him, confused by what I heard, horrified by what seemed his callousness.

"Damn you!" I cursed in a gurgling scream.

I had never spoken to my father so disrespectfully, but I was filled with so much frustration. His ignorance and superstition were like a wall that he had built, one cement block at a time, denying the help that I really needed.

*"Papa!"* I cried out, choking in the blood that was accumulating in my throat, *"no puedes ver. . . que estoy. . . muriendo. . .* can't you see . . . I'm dying!"

My father kept his eyes on my cadaverous legs with that undecipherable smirk on his face. Then he turned and walked away.

"*Papa! Papa! Papa!*" I kept repeating to myself, as rage and fear took a strangle-hold on me.

I heard the pickup motor start up. I knew that in a few moments I would hear the motor whir away, as I often had, and the sound of it would disappear into the distance. He would drive away from this pathetic son – this burden for which he had no remedy.

Mama came into the room and sat on the bed, stroking my arm in her helplessness. Her lips moved in quiet whispers, reciting the litany of *oraciones* that came from her arsenal of prayers.

Then my father reappeared at the door.

He walked to the bed and put the sheets over my legs. He leaned down and heaved my bony, six-foot frame into his arms. He carried me out of the room, through the house and out to the pickup. The passenger door was open and he set me down on the seat. He shut the door, then got into the driver's seat and kicked the motor into gear. We traveled down the road of the camp and onto the main road. We turned south then west. Except for my labored breathing, we trudged toward Delano in silence. The truck chugged into town and the motor stopped in front of the office of a medical doctor – Dr. Williams.

Dad got out of the pickup and came to my side, opened the door and began to scoop my body out of the truck. I protested, wanting to maneuver myself out of the truck. But he shook his head and insisted on taking me into his arms.

I might have been a pile of bones, but I was still a big kid. My father mustered all his strength and heaved me up and I surrendered and allowed myself to be carried into the doctor's office like a newborn baby.

There were a few patients in the waiting room, but when the nurse at the reception desk saw us enter, she immediately directed us into an examination room and my father maneuvered me onto the table. Dr. Williams entered, put his stethoscope to my chest, and within seconds said, "This boy is tubercular. He's practically a dead man."

The doctor turned to my father as he made this declaration. I knew my father understood the doctor's words but I offered the words that had, thus far, gone unspoken.

*"Soy tisico, Papa. Estoy muriendo."* ("I'm sick with tuberculosis, Dad. I'm dying.")

My father's eyes widened in terror at hearing the word *tisico*. This word had only one meaning in Spanish – sure death. It was the word for "consumption," a disease that eats away the lungs. I had tuberculosis, a highly contagious and fatal disease.

There was no medical cure for tuberculosis.

I was a dead man.

I was eighteen years old.

# 16

## *Puertas Azules / The Blue Doors*

AN X-RAY CONFIRMED Dr. Williams's diagnosis. In fact, I was in such an advanced stage of tuberculosis that the disease had already eaten deep cavities into my lungs. The doctor advised that I should be immediately taken to a sanitarium because I was highly contagious. All our cooking utensils and linen at the house should be boiled and the walls and floors swabbed with chlorine. The sooner I was removed from the house, the better. Not only did I start to feel like a discard, like a piece of *basura,* garbage that needed to be disposed of, but my father's panic-stricken expression took away the little hope that I kept hidden in my heart. In my father's world, a hospital was not a place to go for healing; it was a place where you went to die.

Dad and I rode back to the camp in an uncomfortable

silence, almost petrified by fear and disbelief. When we informed Mama about the fact that I would be leaving the house as soon as possible, she commenced to wash and pack my few clothes. Little did we know that those clothes would be immediately burned at my arrival at the hospital.

Dr. Williams referred us to the Tulare County Health Department and we were informed that a bed was reserved for me at Springville Sanitarium. I hugged Mama *adiós* as tears streamed down her face. She held on to me for a long time. I knew she believed that she would never see me again. I hugged my brothers and sisters and I remember thinking that I would not be there to be their big brother.

I waved to the *vecinos* as we made our way through the camp and onto the road. News traveled very quickly in the small community and they all knew where I was going and had come out to bid me farewell. There were a lot of tears and *"Diós te bendiga . . . God bless you,"* shouted out to me. But where was Connie? I didn't see her dear face or any of her family. A heavy veil of depression draped over me as I left the familiar comfort of the labor camp.

With my father at the wheel, our beat-up pickup made its trek through the cornucopia of teeming life – the fields and orchards abundant with fruit and vegetables – while I was on my way to the death house. The pickup coursed its way up the highway, up into the hills and into the mountains. Again, the twists and turns, blind curves, ascents and descents challenged our tired vehicle. Though the scenery was beautiful with oak and moss-covered boulders, with range cattle lazily grazing, and birds of prey soaring on the wind currents, I could only concentrate on what horrors awaited me. A river coursed below us. We followed the curve of a wide hill and when we came around to the other side there loomed before us what looked like a white fortress nestled in the hills.

Our vehicle made its final ascent to our destination. A nurse met us at the front of the hospital with a wheelchair. She had a mask over her nose and mouth and made no effort to greet me or my father. Before she turned to lead me to the entrance of the reception building, my father put his hands on my shoulders and gave a quick squeeze. He didn't say anything to me. I kept my head down, not wanting to meet his eyes. My emotions toward my father were still very mixed. Should I thank him for finally helping me, or should I curse him for waiting so long.

Upon entering the stark building that smelled of disinfectant, loneliness immediately overtook me. Not only did I have no idea what awaited me, but I didn't know a single person. An atmosphere of sterile coldness permeated the building. There was not one friendly voice offering a "hello" or "welcome." But I really didn't care too much because I was so exhausted by the trip and too sad to dwell on the nightmare of it all.

I was put into a room with three beds. Curiously, at the far end of this room was a huge door with two swinging panels painted bright blue. I was alone in the room. A machine was wheeled in and set beside me. A nurse took a long syringe attached to a tube and inserted the needle deep into my side. I screamed. She didn't explain the procedure and so I had no warning about what was being done to me. Once the needle was in place, the nurse turned the machine on and I began to have the sensation that I was suffocating. Just before I thought I would pass out, the machine was turned off and I lay there taking small breaths, panic setting in. I figured out the rhythm of breathing that I would have to concentrate on since I could only take in a small amount of air. Without a word, the nurse removed the needle and walked out of the room with the machine.

I began to perspire profusely. I couldn't get comfortable. If I tried to move, an excruciating pain would shoot through my chest and into my legs. I learned later that the machine had been given the nickname "Melvin" and its function was to pump air into my lungs. Ironically, this air was pumped into me to collapse the lung. The air would form a bubble and if I tried to move, the air bubble would move around pressing onto my vital organs. I never understood the reason for this procedure, but I remember nurses and doctors entering the room, peering over me, taking notes at various intervals, then leaving. No one made any effort to comfort me, explain the procedure, or give me any sign of hope. When I tried to explain how much pain I was experiencing, I was told that they could give me nothing to relieve the discomfort.

Daily, the needle would be inserted into my lungs and, daily, I felt like I was drowning.

I noticed that the other beds would sometimes be occupied by patients. Though it was almost impossible to speak, I feebly tried to make conversation with them. My attempts were usually met with silence. Some time in the night, these patients would disappear. This was perplexing to me – how they would appear, then disappear.

One night I awoke with a start. There was a strange chill in the air. The blue doors were wide open. Two orderlies had placed a patient on a gurney and were rolling the gurney to the blue doors. It was then that I realized what was happening! In horror, I realized that the blue doors led to the outside. The room I was in was on a raised platform. The gurney would be wheeled to the blue doors and then the body of my former roommate would be slipped into an awaiting hearse. The blue doors would then be closed and the hearse would drive away.

I cannot adequately describe the terror that gripped me. I struggled for air as a frightened gasp escaped my mouth. I had been placed in this room because it was decided that I probably would not survive for long. I realized that there were many who had made the decision that I would never leave this hospital alive.

Mixed with my terror was the beginning of a resolution. I wanted to shout out to the world that I was not to be discarded or written off. The world was not going to have its way with me. "I am Alfonso!" I shouted in the hidden recesses of my soul. I made the decision, then and there, that I would never be wheeled into that hearse. I decided, then and there, that I would fight for my life. I made the unfaltering decision that I would not leave through the blue doors.

And I never did.

# 17

## *Odisea / Odyssey*

AFTER MANY WEEKS, a doctor came to me and told me that I would be leaving the "blue room," but that I was still a very sick young man. I was being given a fifty-fifty chance of survival. Before being introduced to "Melvin," I had millions of bacilli in my lungs but, thanks to this machine, the bacilli were now "countable." I was wheeled into another part of the hospital called the "annex," which had a screened porch. Although I was prohibited from getting out of bed, I could look out of the screened windows and see the beautiful green carpet of the hills and the granite trajectories of the mountains. I was told that if – and when – I got better, I could be wheeled onto the porch. I made the porch my goal. I yearned to be set free from the hospital bed that had become like a prison cell for me. If I could not get out of this bed and run through the countryside, I wanted to, at least, feel a cool breeze on my skin and breathe the pure air of the world beyond the sterile annex walls.

I began to see my fight to survive as a kind of journey. I decided to make small attainable goals, little by little, *poco a poco*. I would do whatever it took to get to that screened porch.

I followed directions. Whatever I was told to do, I did, without complaint or resistance. One day I was wheeled into a room with other patients. The orderlies started at one end of the room and began to conduct a procedure in which they had to draw stomach fluids from each patient. A tube had to be inserted into the mouth, down the throat. The tube had to reach the stomach in order to draw out the acid. This was done without any relaxant or anesthesia. Some patients did not do so well. They struggled and gagged and cried. If the orderlies were unsuccessful, the patient would be strapped down and the tube would be inserted through the nose where it would travel up, and then down, into the throat. This seemed to be much more painful – as evidenced by the cries of the tortured protests.

When my turn came, the orderly asked me if I wanted the tube down my throat or through my nose. I took the tube from him and put it into my mouth. Then I began to swallow. As I did so, I kept visualizing the panorama I could see from my bedside window. I gulped and gagged, but in no time the tube had made its way down my throat. The orderly suctioned what he needed. I then took the tube out, *poco a poco*, until the procedure was over. My strategy had worked: one small goal at a time – one step at a time.

After some time in the annex I started to regain a little strength. I also started to regain some of my appetite for food. I started to imagine Mom's delicious meals. It seemed I could taste her homemade *tortillas*, her *caldos* and *taquitos.*

Every morning, breakfast would be carted into the annex at 7:00 sharp. The menu was always the same: an egg, a piece of toast, a cup of oatmeal, and juice. I would eat this breakfast in about half a minute and be hungry for more. I also noticed that some of the patients had not regained an appetite. They seemed skeletal and listless and their meals would go untouched. All the plates would then be carted away, whether they had food on them or not.

One morning I got the nerve to ask a nurse if I could have two eggs with the next morning's meal. "Absolutely not" was her stern reply. Every patient was allotted one egg and that was all. That was the rule. Case closed.

I remembered my mother's logical conclusion that *así es porque así es.* But that wisdom did not ease my appetite.

The next morning I asked the nurse for another egg. She ignored me. Every morning after that I would argue for another egg, in fact, three eggs would be nice. She was becoming very agitated with me. I was soon visited by the hospital nutritionist. She was not happy with me either. "You see," she explained, "that's the way it is, that's the way it has *always* been, and it will *not* change – not as long as *I'm* in charge!"

I continued to ask for more eggs in the morning. One day I was visited by a doctor who wanted me to explain why I was being such a troublemaker.

"Doctor," I countered. "Isn't it a good thing that I'm hungry? Isn't that a sign that I might be getting better?"

"And besides," I continued, "It's not as if you'll be wasting eggs. Haven't you noticed how many eggs go uneaten every day?" I went on to describe to him the number of eggs that were thrown away every morning, and that was just from this ward. I could tell that he had no knowledge of the situation.

"Well, how many eggs do you think you could eat?" he questioned.

I couldn't believe my ears. Had he really heard what I had to say?

"Three. Maybe four," I boldly suggested.

I don't know if the nutritionist was still in charge or not, but the next morning I had four eggs on my plate – and every morning after that!

Though my appetite had improved, I was still on strict bed rest. One day a nurse helped me out of bed and she instructed me to take a few steps. I was still too weak. I struggled to take a few steps and then the coughing set in. I felt disheartened, but talked myself out of giving in to the disappointment. However, soon after, I had earned the privilege of sitting out on the screened porch. I would be wheeled out to the porch after breakfast and would sit, breathing in the fresh air, and taking in the beauty of the view. I so wanted a piece of art paper and some charcoal or pencil to sketch the wondrous shapes and shadings that surrounded me.

I was lonely for a familiar face. I would look out to the long road that wound its way up to the hospital and would imagine the old pickup bumping along, bringing friends and family for a visit.

And one day it did.

Dad and Mom and my younger brothers and sisters were neatly packed into Dad's newly acquired car and took the trip up to Springville to see me. Doctor Williams had informed my father that I was doing better and that the hospital was going to allow short visits. My family would stand on the other side of a screened partition, behind a fence rail, and we'd talk and laugh. Mom would tell me of all the latest gossip at the camp, and Dad would let me know how the growing season was progressing. My arms ached to hug them, especially Mom, but this was strictly forbidden since I was still contagious.

Those visits were few and far between. On one

occasion, I asked Mom to come closer to the screen. Dad had decided to take an expedition around the grounds and my siblings were chasing each other on the lawn.

"Mama, have you seen or heard from Connie?" Even though I asked the question, I already had a feeling that Connie was no longer interested in me. My sisters and some of the girls at the camp had written, but I had received no word from Connie. After my arrival at the sanitarium, and after I began to feel better, mail day was what I lived for. Getting word from home kept my spirits up. However, letters were not coming as often as I would have liked and, so far, nothing had come from Connie.

As soon as I asked the question, Mom's eyes welled up and I knew that I had asked the question that she had hoped I would not ask.

She explained to me that Connie's parents had forbidden her to have anything to do with me. They had convinced her that I was never going to come back from the hospital and, even if I did, I would be an *inválido* for the rest of my life. Mom was brave to share this with me. I knew it was hard for her but she knew that the truth had to be told.

After that bad news I became quite despondent. I don't think it was so much the fact that Connie had let me go, but the fact that her parents might be right. Would I ever recover? Would I be an invalid for the rest of my life?

About six months after getting porch privilege, I was moved to a new ward called Wayside. This ward is where all the *Mexicanos* were grouped. It was here that I started to truly understand the dilemma of those who spoke no English. Large signs had been posted all over the sanitarium grounds instructing that no Spanish be spoken. However, it was here at Wayside, where the *Mexicanos* congregated, that the rule had its most profound consequence. Everywhere else on the grounds the *Mexicanos* had been scattered, and so the impact was not so apparent. But here, at Wayside, the silence was a strong contrast to the wards where the murmurings of the daily routine sifted through the air. It was here, while at Wayside, that I summoned the nerve to approach the chief physician, Dr. Winn.

I didn't hear from Dr. Winn for a while after my attempt to convince him to change the ruling on the language prohibition. One morning, I awoke to find Dr. Winn staring down at me. I was somewhat startled, wondering how long he had been standing there.

"Good morning, Mr. Espinosa."

I was taken aback by his formal greeting. I could not recall ever being called "Mr. Espinosa" by anyone, thus far, in my life.

"Good morning, doctor," I responded.

He continued to stare down at me. His hand was on his chin and his spectacles were balanced on the tip of his nose.

"I have a proposition for you," were his cryptic words.

All kinds of thoughts started to circle in my head. Was the "troublemaker" about to be told to pack his bags and leave the hospital?

Dr. Winn then took a chair and sat beside my bed. I listened intently as he went on to explain that an experimental drug for tuberculosis had been developed and that human "guinea pigs" were needed to test the drug. He had heard that I was quite outspoken and had, single-handedly, changed the feeding policy at the hospital. He told me that, although he could not change the language policy, he was impressed with the courage I showed at approaching him about the situation. When asked to secure volunteers at Springville for the testing of this new drug, my name had immediately come to his mind.

He went on to say that the procedure would be quite painful and would have to continue for at least two months if not longer. He described, step by step, the course that would have to be taken and then told me that he would certainly understand if I declined to volunteer.

"Will it save my life, doctor?" were my hopeful words.

"We don't know, Al. It might save your life or it might have no effect. It might even kill you."

He got up from the chair and wrapped his fingers

around my bone-thin arm.

"Think about it, son, and let me know. You don't have to make an immediate decision."

He started to walk away, but before he got to the foot of the bed, I said, "I'll do it."

Dr. Winn turned and looked at me. There seemed to be no emotion on his face. Then he turned and walked away without another word.

Several months passed before I heard again from Dr. Winn. One evening he visited and told me that the drug would start to be administered the following day. He described what would be happening and I remember my stomach turning with dread with the thought of what I would have to endure.

The next morning, I was wheeled into a room where I would be isolated for several months. A nurse entered with a tray that had a cotton towel draped over it. She rubbed my upper right arm with alcohol. Then she uncovered the tray to reveal a syringe that had a needle that must have been six inches long. Without a word, she began to insert the needle into my arm. She continued to push the needle at least three inches into the muscle of my arm. According to the doctor's description, the needle would have to make contact with the bone before the medicine could be injected and that's exactly where the needle went. I wanted to scream out with everything I had in me as that needle penetrated, but I knew that if I started screaming I might not be able to stop. I clamped my mouth shut. I know panicky noises must have escaped my throat but, somehow, I did not lose control.

The following morning the nurse again entered. She carried the tray covered with the towel. This time my left arm was injected. On the third morning, my right hip was injected. On the fourth, my left hip was injected. On the fifth morning I couldn't believe it when I heard her measured steps coming down the hall. She entered the room as I looked at her in horror. Where was she going to put that needle? She started to prepare my right arm. It was red and swollen. It was so tender that I hadn't been able to sleep on my right side, nor my left. I think I almost fainted when she injected the needle into my right arm once again.

By the end of the first week I wanted to ask the doctor to stop the injections. I couldn't sleep. Not only was I feverish and nauseated, I couldn't find a comfortable sleeping position. My arms and legs were swollen like balloons. When I did sleep, cold sweats and nightmares plagued me. A bowl was set by my head to collect the vomit that came after every unwanted meal. And again, I felt like a prisoner chained to my bed. But when I got ready to summon a nurse to take my message to Dr. Winn, I'd think about the possibility of getting well. Without the drug, the chances were high that the tuberculosis would continue to eat away at my lungs.

It was at about this time that a miracle occurred. I

received a short stack of letters on mail day. One was from my sister, Frances, and one from my brother, Robert. And one was postmarked to Mr. Al Espinosa from Miss Mary Zaragoza. I tore open Mary's letter. As I started to read her beautiful handwritten letter, I remember tears streaming from my eyes. I'm not sure why, but I think it was just the fact of knowing that someone outside the family had remembered that I was still alive. Mary's letter was full of interesting news, a poem, and a joke, and she ended the letter by telling me not to give up. She also wrote that she'd like to continue writing if it was okay with me.

I don't think I would be exaggerating to say that Mary's letter turned everything around for me. Somehow, I continued to endure the injections and, somehow, Mary's letters continued to arrive. In one of her letters she included her photograph. I put the photo in a frame by my bedside and I would look into her smiling face on the days that I didn't think I could go *un paso más.*

After one month of treatment, I was a massive bundle of swollen pain. I would be helped out of bed for once-a-day toilet privilege and weekly x-rays. Every other day I would have to swallow the throat tube to provide the doctors with mucous from my lungs.

After I had endured two months of treatment, Dr. Winn entered the room and walked up to my bed.

"Alfonso," he said with that stern, expressionless

look on his face. "I'm stopping the injections."

This news stirred mixed emotions in me. The thought of another injection would cause much anxiety to well up in me. However, I knew that this drug was my only hope of being healed. Was he here to tell me that all this torture had been for nothing?

"Al, you have made remarkable progress. In my opinion you don't need any more treatments. I think the drug has cured you."

I stared, dumbfounded, at Dr. Winn. Had I heard correctly? Cured?

I had been at Springville for almost two years.

I was going to live.

The drug, streptomycin, would continue to cure people of tuberculosis for many years to come.

# 18

## *La Mancha / The Stain*

ALTHOUGH THE DRUG had stopped the destruction that tuberculosis was causing in my lungs, I still was not ready to leave Springville. I was going to continue to need therapy – pneumatics – to strengthen my lungs, and much rest was still required.

Mary and I continued to exchange letters and she made several visits to see me at the hospital. Sometimes she'd bring her sisters and friends and we'd take short walks. As my strength continued to increase, we would take longer walks and follow the creek that sauntered along the perimeters of the hospital grounds. And, one day, we climbed to the top of a hill. Though winded, I whooped for joy at this accomplishment.

I had earned more privileges, and was not confined in any way. Because I had so much time on my hands,

I made it my goal to read more. Daily, a librarian
would make her rounds throughout the hospital wards,
distributing all kinds of literature and magazines to
those who felt inclined to read. I had always been one
of her better customers and especially loved the comic
books. One day I asked her to suggest a good novel, and
she immediately grabbed a hefty book from the bottom
of the cart. When I saw the size of the book I balked, but
she assured me that if I kept with it I would thoroughly
enjoy the story. The title of the book was *Don Quixote
de La Mancha*. I remember being confused and amazed
when I learned that the original story had been written
in Spanish by a man named Miguel de Cervantes. It was
considered one of the greatest pieces of literature ever
written. Because of the experiences I had had in school,
I think that, subconsciously, I found it hard to believe
that anything of importance had ever been written in the
language of my parents.

I must say that the first few chapters were a
challenge. I struggled with much of the vocabulary
but, after requesting a dictionary and concentrating on
visualizing the story, some magic started to happen.
Before long, I was immersed in the story of a whimsical
man from *La Mancha*, Spain, who dared to live as
his heart led him; who fought the real and imaginary
forces that tried to stop him from accomplishing his
fantastical journey. I laughed and shook my head at his
antics. I cried when he made proclamations that seemed

ludicrous, but touched my heart with their truth. I would read for hours, unable to put the book down. When I finally came to the last page, I sat on the rocker on the porch looking out at the hills and mountains beyond, and I thought about all that I had learned by reading this one book.

I was inspired by the great themes of this story. In his delusion of chivalry, Don Quixote refused to treat anyone with disrespect. He treated all whom he encountered with dignity, no matter their station in life. Along with his trusted steward, he was on a quest to undo all injustice – refusing to accept things as they were.

It was amazing to me that this novel had originally been written in the language of my parents – the language that I had been taught to use with caution and with fear of punishment. I contemplated, not with anger but with sadness, how I had been duped for so long with the lie that the language of my parents, Spanish, was somehow inferior.

I realized I was hungry for knowledge. I looked forward to the library cart as it made its daily rounds. The librarian enthusiastically supplied me with a steady stream of classic literature. One day, impressed with my interest in reading, she handed me several books and told me that they were a gift. One of the books was titled *Plato's Republic*. A second book contained the writings of Aristotle. She gave me a book filled with wonderful poetry. She gave me a Bible. I read the books and kept them next to Mary's portrait on my bedstand.

I had become a voracious reader and, the more I read, that stain of inferiority that I had battled since I was a young child began to vaporize. I was learning great lessons about the struggles of humanity: that what I had suffered and struggled with were the sufferings and struggles of so many who had gone before me. I didn't have a clue what would become of me after I left the sanitarium, but I was no longer fearful. Like Don Quixote, I longed to leave all that confined me and proceed with my life's adventure.

One night, as I lay in my bed, I stared up at the offensive sign over the entrance of the ward that read NO SPANISH ALLOWED. I quietly got out of bed, picked up a chair, positioned it under the sign, got up on the chair and maneuvered the sign off the wall. The next morning I mentioned to some of my ward mates that the sign was no longer on the wall, therefore, it must be all right to speak Spanish. They looked at me, incredulously, as I nodded my head and reassured them. When a nurse entered the ward and heard all the commotion, in Spanish, she turned on her heels and returned with several other nurses who insisted that the talking stop.

"But the sign is gone!" we countered.

Mysteriously, other signs throughout the grounds began to disappear. The next day the signs would be tacked back up, and the following day the signs would be gone again. The maintenance men were kept very busy securing the NO SPANISH ALLOWED signs all over Springville Sanitarium.

I was sitting on my bed reading on one warm afternoon when Dr. Winn entered the ward with several angry nurses. He walked straight to my bed and stood there with his arms crossed in front of him. The nurses gathered around him with pinched faces and angry grimaces.

"Young man, I'm getting many complaints about you. These nurses believe that you are the culprit. Are you the mystery man taking the signs down at this hospital?"

I looked Dr. Winn squarely in the eye. I wanted to deny what the nurses had to say, but I could not lie to Dr. Winn.

"Yes, sir," I said, trying to keep my voice steady. "I'm the thief . . . and as long as I'm here . . . as long as it's possible . . . I'll continue to rip those signs down because it isn't right. These men deserve to be treated with respect. This is a free country and they have the *right* to speak in whatever language they choose."

Several of the nurses rolled their eyes and I could hear the impatient tapping of toes. These were good and dedicated women. They were here to help us get well. I thoroughly appreciated all that they did and I had much respect for them, but they were plain wrong to insist that we refrain from speaking the language of our birth.

I kept my eyes steadily on Dr. Winn. I was not going to back down.

Dr. Winn stared back at me with that face that never seemed to show emotion. I could not read his thoughts. The furrow between his eyes deepened. Then, he turned and walked to the entrance of the ward. He grabbed a chair and positioned it under the sign that had been nailed back onto the wall. He got up on the chair, grabbed the sign and with a mighty heave, ripped it from the wall and threw it down. It skidded across the floor. The nurses backed away in surprise and confusion. Then Dr. Winn got off the chair, dusted off his coat, and walked out of the ward.

The next day the offensive signs were removed from the grounds at Springville.

They never went up again.

# Epilogue

My name is Yolanda. My father was Alfonso Cruz Espinosa. I listened to my father's stories and remembered them.

I found it amazing that my father survived the many challenges that life put in his way – not only the disease and the stark poverty that he was helpless to circumvent in his youth, but the ignorant hatred that he endured; the blatant racism that peppered his life. But always, there to guide his way, were the good people – those who encouraged him, who shared their skills and intelligence, their gentle wisdom and faith, who gave him the courage to continue on his journey, his caracol, one step at a time.

My father used to tell me a story. This story was about a man who was not content with his life. "My life has been too hard!" he would shout to the heavens. "My cross is too heavy!"

This man was taken to a great valley where many crosses were planted in the ground. A voice from above thundered, "Choose your cross!" The man perused the many crosses. Some were smaller but rough and splintered, and some were larger. Some were massive.

*When he looked again at the cross that he carried on his shoulder, he realized that his cross was not so bad. In fact, he realized that he preferred to carry the cross that he had carried all along. "This cross will do fine," he said to himself as he continued on his journey.*

My father left Springville Sanitarium in 1947 at the age of twenty-one. He left with no viable skills except for his speedy proficiency at typing with two fingers – a skill he acquired in order to type his long letters to Mary. He also left with the great wisdom and language skills that he gleaned from the classic literature that the hospital librarian had shared with him.

Before leaving the sanitarium, the doctors gave my father strict orders not to return to the fields. The sulfur and other contaminants would irritate his lungs, which were still in the process of healing. He was directed to the Tulare County Department of Rehabilitation. The results of an I.Q. test showed that he could take any career path he chose. He could be an engineer, teacher, architect or lawyer, but my father had no high school diploma and no money. His own father had no means to help him.

The Department of Rehabilitation offered my father two years of vocational training and he chose to attend business classes in Porterville, California.

While he was in Porterville, he received a letter

from Mary. The city of Delano was looking for a clerk and interpreter for the police department. The pay was not much, but would he happen to know of anyone who would be interested in the job. Evidently, there had been an altercation between the police and a Mexican-American resident. The Hispanic community had become agitated with some of the actions taken by the police and had stormed city hall with their protests. The city council had decided that the city needed someone with bilingual skills to help with communication between the department and the Hispanic residents.

My father borrowed a friend's car and drove to Delano to talk to the chief of police, not really thinking he, himself, was qualified for the position.

He was hired on the spot.

Two days later he began his duties at the front desk. His main duties as a clerk were to greet people, interpret when needed, and file the reports generated by the officers.

Up to this point, all police reports had been handwritten, since none of the police officers knew how to type. My father described the difficulty he had filing the police reports. In trying to decipher the cryptic handwriting of the policemen, he was surprised to find that their spelling and grammar were atrocious, as well.

A sergeant by the name of Charles McNutt noticed my father's language skills and saw that he typed his own memos. Sergeant McNutt asked my father if he would be willing to edit and type *his* police reports. Soon, all the policemen were coming to my father to have their reports edited and typed. As he carefully prepared these reports, he was vicariously learning the technicalities of the law enforcement profession.

A new policeman was hired to work the night shift. This young man was put on patrol with a veteran officer. The older officer would enter the front office quite frustrated with this new recruit, who would often fall asleep as soon as the night patrol began. This was becoming a regular occurrence. One evening, the veteran officer entered the front office, extremely agitated, and walked into the office of the chief. Then the two walked out of the building together. My father knew that the rookie was in big trouble.

The chief found the young officer fast asleep in the patrol car and fired him as he snored away. The chief then re-entered the office and walked up to my father.

"Would you like to be a cop?"

My father, not believing his ears, nodded his head in the affirmative. The chief pinned a badge on him and handed him a holster and a gun!

The year was 1951, and that is how my father's career as a police officer began.

He was the first police officer of Mexican ancestry on the Delano police force.

Because my father had never graduated from high school, he took night classes and received his General Education Diploma. He studied law enforcement handbooks and started to go up the ranks in the police department because he was earning the highest scores on qualifying exams. This fact was somewhat perplexing to the veteran policemen who struggled through the examinations. This fact was quite agitating to some in city government who were very biased against minorities in this era prior to the Civil Rights Movement. My father received a letter from a city manager that assured him that no Mexican would *ever* reach the top ranks in the department.

My father was promoted to sergeant in July of 1958.

He became a lieutenant in 1961.

In 1963, with the highest qualifying scores, my father, Alfonso Cruz Espinosa, became Captain of Police, second in command, of the Delano Police Department.

A year before becoming a patrolman, my father married my mother, Mary Zaragoza. They exchanged wedding vows on August 20, 1950, and eventually settled into a house on Clinton Street in Delano. I was born in 1952. My sister, Rosemary, was born in 1955.

My parents became very active in their community. Voter registration drives, neighborhood improvement projects, local and national campaigns, and cultural events were just some of the many endeavors they undertook to improve the lot of *los Mexicanos.*

Even before their marriage, they helped to organize a protest to desegregate the movie theater in Delano. During World War II, my uncle Manuel served in Germany and fought in the Battle of the Bulge. My uncle Robert served as a Marine in the Pacific and fought in the battle for Okinawa. Yet, when they returned home they were denied entrance into the main hall of the movie theater. They were asked to go to the balcony with the other minorities. Another veteran by the name of Daniel Melendez was also denied entrance. They, along with my parents and others, rallied to fight this injustice. After several organized protests, the minorities of Delano attained their right, as United States citizens, to sit wherever they pleased.

In 1965, the Grape Strike, also known as *La Huelga* started in Delano. Cesar Chavez, the leader of the strike, met with my parents in their home, asking them to become leaders in the strike. He expressed his respect for the in-roads my parents had made as pioneers in the struggle for equality for the Mexican-American community. Cesar explained that there would be public demonstrations that would cause heated confrontations. He warned that the police would be put in a defensive position. Cesar wanted my father to leave the police department and join the strike.

My parents declined Cesar's offer to become

involved with the strike. My father had worked hard to sustain his career as a law-enforcement officer and wanted to continue in his hard-earned profession. He wanted to continue to serve the many that came seeking *El Capitan,* the captain, with their legal concerns and dilemmas.

Senate Hearings on the farm labor problem were held in Delano in 1966 and major demonstrations were expected. After the event, which attracted national attention, the Chief of Police received a letter from one of the organizers who was sympathetic to the Grape Strike. The letter came from a Catholic priest, Roger Mahoney.

In the letter, the Reverend thanked the police department for "kindness and assistance" and commended the department for its "outstanding job in handling the entire situation." He wrote, "In particular, may I single out Captain Espinosa, who aided us in many ways during the three-day event." This young priest would later become Cardinal Roger Mahoney, Archbishop of the Diocese of Los Angeles.

In 1976, my father was offered the position of Executive Director of the Republican National Hispanic Assembly in Washington, D.C. He accepted, and left his job as policeman after having served for twenty-seven years.

On May 24, 1976, a press release in the *Bakersfield Californian,* a local newspaper, stated, "Espinosa will direct efforts . . . to place Spanish-speaking Americans in key government posts. The appointment makes him one of the top ranking Mexican-Americans in the nation."

On a warm June day in 1976, I waved goodbye to my parents as they drove away, loaded down with their suitcases and various household items. With my father at the wheel, the car turned southward onto the freeway. Along the way, the road signs read *Pond, McFarland, Wasco, Lerdo.* He was leaving behind the valley communities and labor camps that had all been part of his life's journey – *Delano, Richgrove, The California Ranch, Tulare, Hanford, Springville, Porterville.*

He could not help but remember the constant moving that had wearied him as a youth. He smiled at the happy irony of yet another journey.

My parents started their ascent up the Grapevine, *El Caracol,* which was no longer the treacherous path of long ago. Behind them lay the Great Valley. Their car hummed along the six-lane interstate, with diesels climbing upward and sports cars whizzing by. They kept a steady speed as they entered and traveled through the great metropolis – the City of the Angels. They turned eastward and continued on their journey across the country. A week later they entered our nation's capital – Washington, D.C.

A few days later, on the Fourth of July, 1976, the

Bicentennial of this nation's birth, my parents watched in awe as hundreds of brilliant fireworks burst in the night sky – glittering starbursts reflecting in the waters of the Potomac. The Washington Monument and the Lincoln Memorial stood majestic below the multicolored explosions that sparkled like stars in the eyes of thousands of spectators. My father could not help but remember the stories of his own father as a young shepherd boy in Mexico, peering into the night sky so very long ago, as myriad stars illumined the heavens.

The little boy from the labor camp would now be shaking hands with presidents, senators and congressmen. The little boy, whose hands had been rapped for speaking Spanish, would now be conferring in Spanish with Hispanics from all over the nation.

My parent's stay in Washington was exciting and busy, but short-lived. My mother had been battling cancer and was in remission when they left Delano. The cancer returned and she came home to Delano to be close to her doctors and family. My father returned from Washington to help her through her illness.

My mother died in 1980.

In 1987, my mother was posthumously honored as one of Kern County's "Movers and Shakers." A caption below her photograph in the publication noted that, "Mary Espinosa was an early role model for Hispanics in Delano and was noted for her ability to work with all segments of the community in creating better understanding of the needs of minorities."

My father died in June of 1990, at the age of sixty-three, after also battling cancer. As the funeral procession coursed its way from St. Mary's Church in Delano to the cemetery, police officers halted traffic at each intersection. As the hearse carrying my father's coffin slowly processed by, they stood at attention and saluted.

Before my father passed away, he was in a coma for several days. I don't know what thoughts, if any, were visiting him in this quiet state, but I choose to believe that before he took his last breath, *he was once again a little boy sitting at his mama's table, swinging his legs and eating his warm* avena, *while she hummed and rolled the* palote.

# El Caracol

## A poem by Alfonso Cruz Espinosa

It's quiet now, oh, so quiet, so very quiet.
But it gives chance to turn around and look from where I came.
From yonder mountains and far beyond I came, very young –
oh, so very young.

Years before, only a trail, a path perhaps, that's all it was.
Gravel here and there, treacherous curves, climbs and declines.

And, I remember so very well, foot paddles and screeching brakes,
Grinding metal until it was safe, momentarily, till it was time to
climb again.

Por Diós! Qué es esto?
In such a young mind, a bold impression.
A deep wide hole in the ground below, as far as the eye could see.

"El Valle," I heard my parents say, "El Valle San Joaquin!"

But to get there, first the caracol.

And again the winding curves, steeper still, and again the brakes.
The fear, the uncertainty and another curve and still another.

My father, my mother, their faces, pale fear.

Twisting and turning, my dad with all his faith in what he held.
And Mama con su "Jesus, Maria y Jose!"

Finally the calm arrived and the going was now not so bad.

I glimpsed behind from where I came, El Caracol.

Now it was behind, or so it seemed,
For how was I to know so young of mind that . . .
The caracol was yet to come.

# Spanish / English Glossary

## A

Adiós [ah-thee-OS], goodbye; go with God.

Atole [ah-TOH-leh], thick warm drink made from cornmeal, sugar, and cinnamon

Avena [ah-VE-nah], oatmeal/warm cereal

"Ay, Diós mio!" [i-ee/dee-os/mee-o], "Oh, my God!"

## B

Barrio [BA-rree-o], ethnic (Hispanic) neighborhood

Burrito de huevo [boo-RREE-to/deh/oo-ay-vo], egg rolled in a tortilla

## C

Café de canela [ka-FEH/deh/kah-NEH-la], cinnamon-flavored coffee

Chihuahua [Chee-WAH-wah], a state in northern Mexico

Colonia [ko-LO-nee-ah], Hispanic "colony" or neighborhood

Comal [ko-MAHL], flat iron or earthenware platter for cooking tortillas

"Cóme, mi hijíto" [KOH-meh/mee/ee-HEE-toh], "Eat, my son."

## D

"Diós te bendiga" [dee-os/te//ven-DEE-gah], "God bless you."

## E

El Valle [VA-yeh], the valley

   Joaquin [wah-KEEN]; Allende [ah-YEN-deh]

El Alacrán [Ah-la-KRAHN], the Scorpion, Scorpio.

**F**

Frijoles al'olla [free-HO-les/ahl/O-yah], beans from a pot

**G**

Grito [GREE-toh], high-pitched shout

**H**

Hacienda [ah-see-EN-dah], landowner's estate; ranch

**L**

La Bufa [BOO-fah], vent in the earth; mine

La Conquista [kon-KEE-stah], referring to the Spanish conquest of Mexico in the 16th century.

La Huevona [weh-VO-nah], slang: The Lazy One

La Reina [RAY-nah], the Queen; referring to the mother of Jesus

La Virgen [VEER-hen], referring to Mary, the mother of Jesus

Los jefes [HE-fez], the bosses; supervisors

**M**

Mexican [MEK-si-kin], American English pronunciation for a native of Mexico

Mexicano [meh-hee-KA-no], Spanish pronunciation for a native of Mexico

**O**

Oraciones [oh/rah/see/OH/nes], prayers

**P**

Padrino [pah-DRREE-noh], godfather; sponsor

Paisano [pa-ee-SAH-noh], fellow countryman

Palote [pah-LO-the], wooden rolling pin for making tortillas

## S

San Francisco del Oro [Sahn/frahn-SEES-ko/dehl/O-ro], Saint
   Francis "of the Gold"
Señor [sehn-YOR], Mister; Sir

## T

Tamales [tah-MAH-les], meat wrapped in cornmeal and corn husks
Taquitos de carne [tah-KEE-tos/deh/KAR-neh], meat rolled in
   tortillas
Tisico [TEE-see-koh], slang: tuberculosis/consumption/lung
   disease
Tortillas [tor-TEE-ahs], flat round bread of corn or flour

## V

Vecinos [veh-SEE-nos], neighbors
Villa [VEE-yah], village or large house
   Santa Barbara [sahn-tah/BAR-bah/rah]
Virgen de Guadalupe [VEER-hen/deh/goo-ah-dah-LOO-peh],
   Virgin Mary of Guadalupe, who is very special to Hispanic
   Catholic culture

*Alfonso at his first job as desk clerk, 1949. Delano Police Department*

*Patrolman, 1954. Delano Police Department*

*The author with her father, 1955. Delano, California*

*Alfonso with Vice President Nelson D. Rockefeller,*
*Republican National Convention, Kansas City, 1976*

*Rita and Alfonso, Sr., c. 1950's*

*Alfonso at Springville Sanitarium,
after being healed of tuberculosis*

*Alfonso with the "Mexicanos" at Wayside Ward, Springville*

*Al and Mary, 1949.
Delano, California*

*Alfonso ('Fonso)
2 years old
Los Angeles, California*

*Alfonso's bed stand at Springville Sanitarium. Mary's
portrait and his books*

# *About the Author*

YOLANDA ESPINOSA ESPINOZA graduated from San Jose State University with a masters degree in Art History/Cultural Anthropology. During her teaching career, she taught art history and social studies. She is now retired and lives in Baja California, Mexico, with her husband.

Breinigsville, PA USA
23 March 2011
258281BV00001B/62/P